SACRAMENTO PUBLIC LIBRARY

D0622565

WITHDRAWN FROM COLLECTION
OF SACRAMENTO PUBLIC LIBRARY

Why Why Why do tornadoes spin?

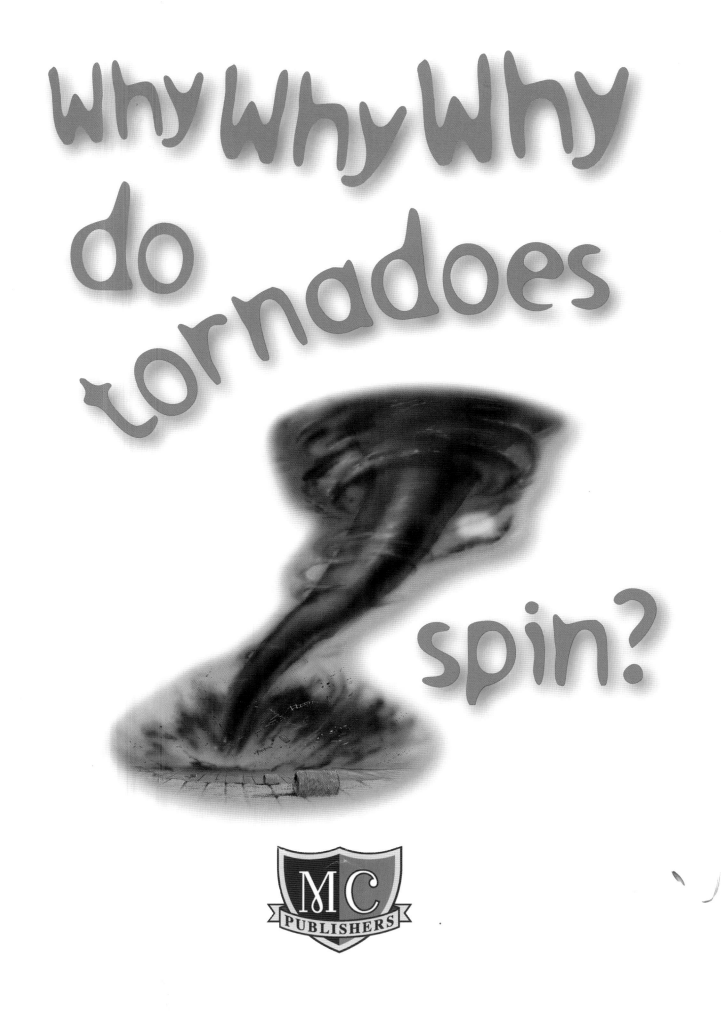

MC PUBLISHERS

First published as hardback in 2006 by Miles Kelly Publishing Ltd, Bardfield Centre, Great Bardfield, Essex, CM7 4SLCopyright © Miles Kelly Publishing Ltd 2006

This 2009 edition published and distributed by:

Mason Crest Publishers Inc.
370 Reed Road, Broomall, Pennsylvania 19008
(866) MCP-BOOK (toll free)
www.masoncrest.com

Why Why Why—
Do Tornadoes Spin?
ISBN 978-1-4222-1586-9
Library of Congress Cataloging-in-Publication data is available

Why Why Why—?
Complete 23 Title Series
ISBN 978-1-4222-1568-5

No part of this publication may be reproduced in whole or in part, or stored in a retrieval system, or transmitted in any form or by any means, electronic, mechanical, photocopying, recording, or otherwise, without written permission from the publishers.

Printed in the United States of America

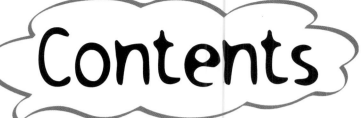

Contents

Why is summer warm and sunny?

The Earth is tipped to one side as it moves round the Sun. Some of the year, the north half of the Earth faces the Sun. Then the Sun is higher in the sky, making the weather warm. This is summer. When the southern half of the Earth faces the Sun, it is winter in the north.

Spring in the north

Summer in the north

The Sun

Why are days longer in summer?

Summer days are longer because the Earth is tilted and spins round. In summer, the Sun rises earlier and sets later. This makes daytime last longer than night. In the middle of summer in Sweden it is light for 21 hours!

Winter in
the north

Why do leaves fall in autumn?

Autumn (Fall) comes between summer and
winter. Many trees lose their leaves in
autumn because it is hard for them to grow
in the dark winter months. The leaves turn
from green to red, orange or brown.
Then they fall to the ground.

Autumn in the north

Find

Can you find
photographs of red,
orange, and brown
leaves in autumn?

Sunshine at midnight!

At the North and South
Poles, the Sun never sets in
summer. It is light all day. In
winter, the Sun never rises.
Then it is dark all day long!

What is the sunniest place?

The Sahara Desert in North Africa is the sunniest place on Earth. It is sunny for nearly 12 hours every day! It hardly rains, which makes it hard for plants and animals to live here. People dress in loose clothes to stop being sunburnt.

Sea makes fire!

Water flowing around the sea can change the weather. El Niño is a warm water current in the Pacific Ocean. Scientists think that this could cause droughts.

When is a lake not a lake?

When it's a mirage! A mirage often happens on a hot day. Hot air near the ground makes light from the bright sky bend upwards. This makes it seem as if there is a lake on the ground in the distance. Really the ground is dry!

Dust storm

People living in the desert

Remember

Can you remember why desert people wear loose clothes, even when it is very hot?

What happens when it doesn't rain?

Sometimes it is dry for a long time in places where it normally rains a lot. This is called a drought. There was a drought in the United States in the 1930s. Crops didn't grow and fields turned to dust. Many people had to leave their farms.

Does Earth have a blanket?

Planet Earth

Yes, it does. The Earth is wrapped in a thick blanket of air. It is called the atmosphere. This is where all the weather happens. The atmosphere also helps to keep the Earth's surface warm at night. In the day it protects us from harmful rays coming from the Sun.

Where does it rain every day?

In a tropical rain forest the weather is always very hot and very wet. The Sun shines every day, and there are downpours of heavy rain, too. Rain forest plants grow very quickly in this steamy weather.

Monsoon downpour!

In some countries it pours with rain for a few weeks every year. This is called a monsoon. In India, enough rain falls in one year to cover the ground with water 85 feet deep!

How deep is the atmosphere?

The atmosphere stretches hundreds of miles above our heads. If you go up through the atmosphere, the air gets thinner and thinner. High up in mountains, mountaineers find it difficult to breathe so they take breathing equipment with them.

Mountaineer

Look

Look at the picture of the Earth above. What do you think the white swirly patterns are?

Where does rain come from?

Most rain comes from the sea! Some seawater turns to gas in the air. If the air rises, the gas becomes water drops. These make clouds. If the drops get big enough, they fall as rain. The water flows back to the sea.

3. Rain falls

2. Water from plants rises into air

4. Water runs into rivers

1. Seawater rises into air

The water cycle

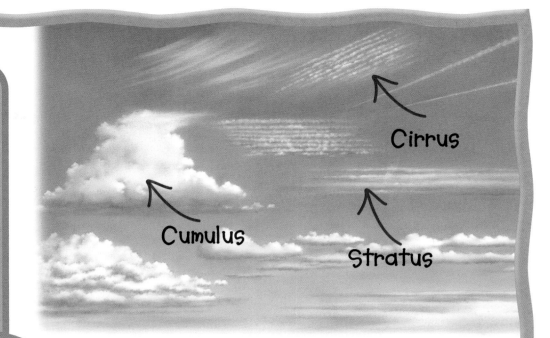
Cirrus

Cumulus

Stratus

Head in the clouds!

The tops of tall mountains are often in the clouds. At the top it looks misty. Mountaineers sometimes get lost in these clouds!

Are all clouds small and fluffy?

Clouds come in lots of different shapes and sizes. Weather experts give the different clouds names. Fluffy clouds are called cumulus clouds. Some are small and some are giant. Flat clouds are called stratus clouds. Wispy clouds high in the sky are called cirrus clouds.

What rain never lands?

Sometimes rain that falls from a cloud never reaches the ground. If the drops of rain fall into very dry air, the water in them turns into gas. This means that the drops disappear and never reach the ground.

Look

Look at the clouds outside today. Are they fluffy or flat? The picture above will help you.

What happens in a flood?

Sometimes a lot of rain falls in a few hours. So much water flows into rivers that they fill up and burst their banks. The rivers flood the land on each side. Sometimes houses disappear under the flood water.

Floods of tears!

The river Nile in Egypt floods every year. Thousands of years ago, the Egyptians made up a story about the flood. It said that a goddess called Isis cried so much that the river filled up with her tears.

Did Noah build an ark?

The Bible tells the story of a man called Noah. He built a great boat called an ark to escape a flood. We don't know if Noah's ark existed. Scientists have found out that there probably was a huge flood thousands of years ago.

Noah's ark

Flooded house

Find

Can you find the country of Egypt and the river Nile in an atlas?

Can there be a flood in a desert?

Yes there can. Most of the time there is no rain in a desert. The hot Sun bakes the ground hard. Once in a while, it rains heavily. The water flows off the ground instead of soaking in. This can cause a flood.

What is snow made of?

Snow is made of ice, which is water that has frozen. When it is very cold in a cloud, tiny bits of ice (crystals) begin to form, instead of water drops. The pieces clump together to make snowflakes that fall to the ground. The weather must be very cold for snow to fall. If it is too warm, the snowflakes melt and turn to rain.

Shiver!

Antarctica is the coldest place on Earth. The lowest temperature ever recorded there is −129°F. That's much, much colder than inside a freezer!

Snow drifts

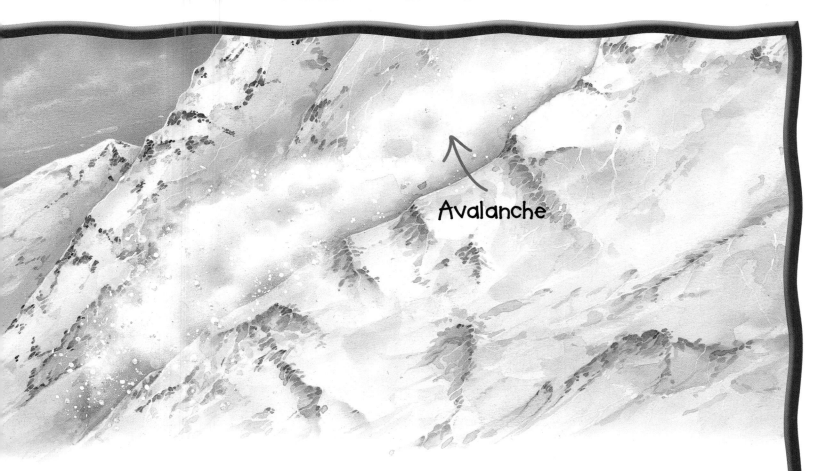

Avalanche

When is snow dangerous?

When lots of snow falls on mountains, deep layers build up on the slopes. The snow may suddenly slide down the mountain. This is an avalanche. A big avalanche can bury a town. A loud noise or even a person walking on the snow can start an avalanche.

Are all snowflakes the same?

It's hard to believe, but all snowflakes are different—even though there are millions and millions of them. This is because every ice crystal in a snowflake has its own shape. No two crystals are the same. Most ice crystals in snowflakes looks like stars with six points.

Think

Can you think why it could be dangerous to ski across a steep hillside covered with snow?

Do tornadoes spin?

Inside a tornado. A tornado is like a spinning funnel made of air. They reach down from giant thunderstorms. The winds can blow at 300 miles an hour. That's twice as fast as an express train! Tornadoes can rip trees from the ground and destroy houses.

Tornado →

Which storm has an eye?

A hurricane is a giant spinning storm made up of super-strong winds. The center is a hole called the eye. Here it is calm and sunny. If a hurricane reaches land, the winds can damage buildings and heavy rain causes floods. Hurricane hunters are planes that fly into hurricanes to measure the wind speed.

Eye

Hurricane hunter

Stormy names!

A tropical storm that starts in the Atlantic Ocean is called a hurricane. In the Pacific Ocean, a tropical storm is called a typhoon. In the Indian Ocean it is called a cyclone.

Draw

Look at the pictures on this page. Can you draw a picture of a tornado and a hurricane?

How do we measure wind?

We measure the wind on a scale called the Beaufort Scale. The slowest wind is Force 1 on the scale. This is called a light breeze. The strongest wind is Force 12. This is called a hurricane. Force zero means there is no wind at all.

What makes the sky clap?

A thunderstorm! Inside a big thundercloud, water drops and bits of ice move up and down, bumping into each other. This makes electricity build up. When the electricity jumps around, we see a spark of lightning and hear a loud clap of thunder.

Huge hail!

Hail is made up of lumps of ice called hailstones. Hail can fall from thunderclouds. The biggest hailstone ever fell in Bangladesh in 1986. It was the size of a grapefruit!

When is lightning like a fork?

When lightning jumps from a thundercloud to the ground, it looks like huge forks in the sky. If lightning jumps from one cloud to another, the clouds light up. This is called sheet lightning. Lightning can be red, blue, yellow, or white.

Lightning

Does lightning hit buildings?

Lightning often hits tall buildings. The buildings have a metal spike on top called a lightning conductor. When lightning hits a building, the lightning conductor carries the electricity to the ground. If there was no lightning conductor, the building could be damaged by the lightning.

Thundercloud

Count

Count the seconds between a flash of lightning and a clap of thunder. The bigger the number, the further away the thunderstorm.

What is a rainbow made of?

Rainbow

A rainbow is made of sunlight. The light bounces through raindrops. This splits the light into different colors. The colors of a rainbow are always the same. They are red, orange, yellow, green, blue, indigo, and violet.

Northern lights

Remember

Can you remember all seven colors of a rainbow?

When does the sky have drapes?

In the far north and the far south of the world, amazing patterns of light sometimes appear in the sky. They look like colorful drapes. The patterns are called auroras (or-roar-rers). They happen when tiny light particles from the Sun smash into the air.

Rainbow with no color!

A fogbow is a rainbow that is white. You might see a fogbow when the Sun shines through fog. It is white because the water drops in fog are too small to split up the light into rainbow colors.

When can you see three suns?

If there are thin clouds high in the sky, you might see three suns. The clouds are made of bits of ice. These bend light from the Sun. This makes it look as if there are two extra suns in the sky. We call these mock suns, or sun dogs.

What is a rain dance?

In many hot places, such as Africa, it only rains once or twice a year. People may dance traditional rain dances if the rain does not fall. In the past, people believed that rain dances really could bring clouds and rain.

Who first recorded the weather ?

Over 3,000 years ago in China, people made notes about the weather. They studied how windy it was, or if it rained or snowed. They carved the information onto pieces of tortoiseshell.

Rain dance

Are weather sayings true?

There are many sayings about the weather. Most of them are true. One saying is "Clear Moon, frost soon." If there are no clouds in the sky you can see the Moon clearly. It also means it will get cold quickly at night. So the saying is true.

Full Moon

Weather cows!

Some people think that cows lie down when it is going to rain. But this weather saying is not true. Cows lie down on sunny days, too!

Discover

Can you find some more sayings about the weather? You could ask your teacher, or try looking in a book.

Which bird spins in the wind?

A metal cockerel on a weather vane. The cockerel spins so it can point in any direction. When the wind blows, the cockerel spins and points to where the wind is coming from. If the wind is blowing from the north, it is called a north wind. The wind blows from the north, south, east, and west.

Weather vane

Groundhog Day!

February 2 is called Groundhog Day. If people see an animal called a groundhog, they think that it will stay cold for another six weeks!

What is a weather house?

A weather house is a model that can tell how much moisture is in the air. If it is going to be dry, a lady in summer clothes comes out. If it is going to be rainy, a man with an umbrella comes out.

Weather house

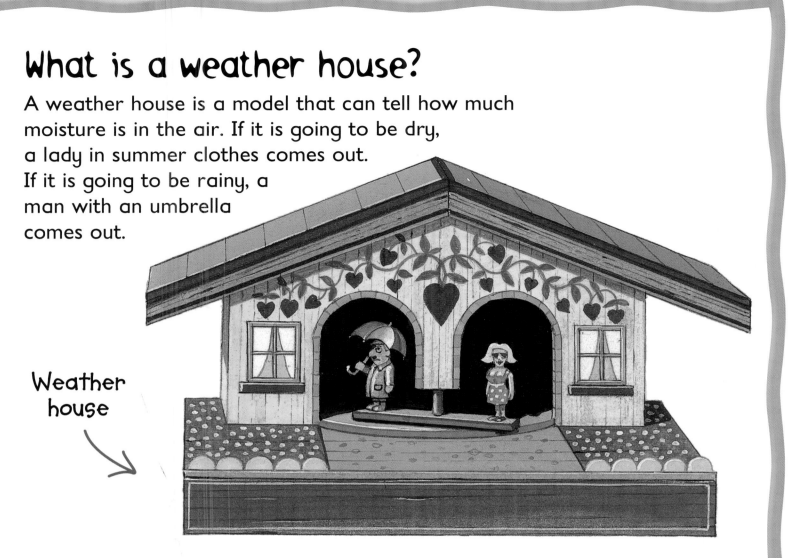

How do we know how hot it is?

By reading a thermometer. A thermometer shows the temperature, which is how hot the air around us is. The first thermometer was made in 1714 by Gabriel Daniel Fahrenheit.

Think

From which direction does a southerly wind blow? North or south?

Can planes tell the weather?

Weather planes don't carry any passengers. Instead they fly through the air recording the weather. They measure the temperature of the air, the speed of the wind and how much water is in the air. This information helps weather forecasters tell us what the weather is going to be like.

Weather plane

Astronaut snaps!

Astronauts who travel on the space shuttle and live on space stations take cameras with them. They often take amazing photographs of clouds and thunderstorms from space.

Why do scientists fly balloons?

Scientists fly balloons to find out about the weather. The balloons are filled with a gas called helium. They float up through the air and carry instruments that measure the weather. The information is sent back to the ground by radio.

Weather balloon

Remember

Can you remember how information gets from a weather balloon down to the ground?

How do we watch weather from space?

With weather satellites. A satellite moves around the Earth in space. It takes photographs of the clouds below and sends them back to Earth. Satellite photographs show which way hurricanes are moving. They help forecasters to warn people if a hurricane is heading their way.

Did weather kill the dinosaurs?

Dinosaurs lived millions of years ago. Scientists think that they may have died because the weather all over the world got colder. They think this happened when a giant rock (meteorite) from space hit the Earth. This threw lots of dust into the air, which blocked out the Sun.

Meteorite hitting the Earth

Is Greenland green?

Greenland is a big island in the Atlantic Ocean. It is covered with a thick sheet of ice. Hundreds of years ago, Greenland was green because it was not so cold and icy. People from northern Europe called Vikings farmed there. They moved away when the weather got colder.

Vikings in Greenland

Windy tower!

The Tower of Winds is a tower in Athens, Greece. It was built 2,000 years ago. It had a giant wind vane on top to measure the direction of the wind.

Find

Can you find Greenland on a map of the world?

Is our weather changing?

Weather experts think the weather is getting warmer. This might be happening because we are cutting down forests. When trees are burned, they release a gas called carbon dioxide. This traps heat from the Sun in the atmosphere.

Quiz time

Do you remember what you have read about weather? These questions will test your memory. The pictures will help you. If you get stuck, read the pages again.

1. Why do leaves fall in autumn?

page 5

2. When is a lake not a lake?

page 7

3. Where does it rain every day?

page 8

4. How deep is the atmosphere?

page 9

5. Are all clouds small and fluffy?

page 11

6. What rain never lands?

page 11

7. What happens in a flood?

page 12

8. Did Noah build an ark?

page 13

9. When is snow dangerous?

page 15

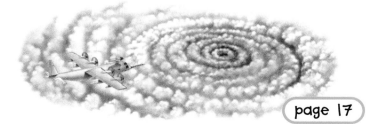

10. Which storm has an eye?

page 17

11. What makes the sky clap?

page 18

12. Who first recorded the weather?

page 22

13. What is a rain dance?

page 22

Answers

1. Because it is hard for them to grow in the dark winter months
2. When it's a mirage
3. In a tropical rain forest
4. Hundreds of miles
5. No, they come in different shapes and sizes
6. Drops that fall into very dry air
7. A lot of rain falls and floods the land
8. We don't know if Noah's ark existed
9. In an avalanche
10. A hurricane
11. A thunderstorm
12. The Chinese
13. A traditional dance to bring on clouds and rain

Index

QC884.2 .D4 F54 2009
Fleck, John, 1959-
The tree rings' tale

D0687405

SCARDED

Colorado Mountain College
Quigley Library
3000 County Road 114
Glenwood Springs, CO 81601

THE TREE RINGS' TALE

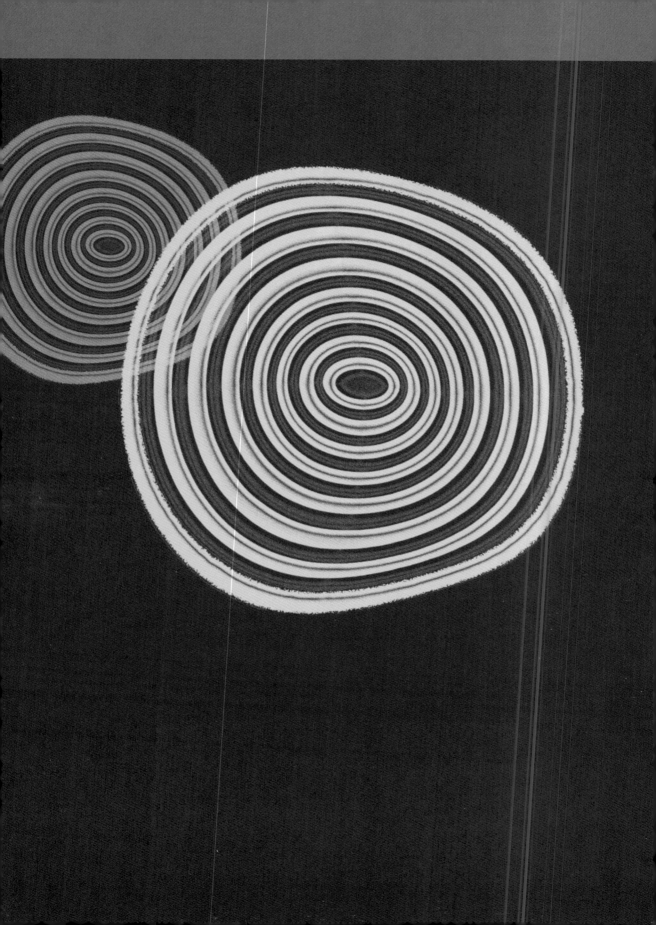

THE
Tree Rings' Tale

Understanding Our Changing Climate

JOHN FLECK

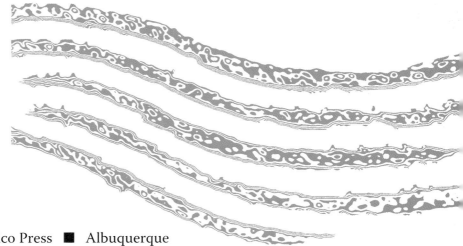

University of New Mexico Press ■ Albuquerque

Barbara Guth Worlds of Wonder

Science Series for Young Readers

Advisory Editors: David Holtby and Karen Taschek
Please see page 87 for more information about the series.

© 2009 by John Fleck
All rights reserved. Published 2009
Printed in Singapore

13 12 11 10 09   1 2 3 4 5

LIBRARY OF CONGRESS CATALOGING-IN-PUBLICATION DATA

Fleck, John, 1959–
The tree rings' tale : understanding our changing climate / John Fleck.
p. cm. — (Barbara Guth Worlds of wonder science series for young readers)
Includes index.
ISBN 978-0-8263-4757-2 (hardcover : alk. paper)
1. Dendroclimatology.
2. Paleoclimatology.
3. Climatic changes—History.
I. Title.
QC884.2.D4F54 2009
551.6—dc22
2009001692

Designed and typeset by Mina Yamashita.
Text composed in Warnock Pro, an Adobe Originals font
designed by Robert Slimbach. Display composed in
Frutiger 77 Black Condensed designed by Adrian Frutiger in 1976.
Printed by TWP, Inc.

To Lissa Heineman,

for sharing my great adventure

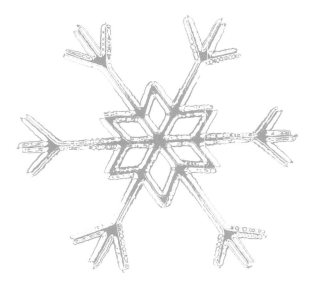

Contents

John Wesley Powell.

Preface

Science, physicist Richard Feynman said, is "the great adventure of our time." Beyond being fun, science also has important things to tell us about how to live our lives. We live in a land with little water. The science that can help us make sense of that fact is very important indeed.

The science in this book doesn't fit into any neat scientific cubbyhole. It's the science of the oceans and the weather and the history of rocks and mountains. The study of ancient people and the stars figures into the story. It's also about the adventures of scientists trying to understand how our world works.

The story for me started with a pair of biologists who showed me what scientists call the tree ring record. Its distinctive squiggles, a record of how trees grow during wet and dry years, show climate changing over thousands of years. I never forgot those squiggles.

Those biologists were passionate about what the tree rings have to tell us. The West can be wet for years at a time. But sooner or later, it always dries out, and it stays that way for years at a time. Since that chance meeting with those two biologists, I have met many scientists who think this is one of the key things about climate we need to know.

The science of tree rings hadn't been invented when explorer John Wesley Powell made his epic trips down the Colorado River in the 1800s. But he noticed the way the river rose and fell. Eventually, he realized how important that was for people trying to live in the West. This story begins and ends with Powell. It's also a story of people like Julio Betancourt, the Cuban-born scientist who as a young man crawled over the cliffs at Chaco Canyon. He was looking for the pack rat middens that changed our understanding of how climate had changed. It's a story of people like Connie Woodhouse, whose travels to the mountains of the Four Corners states to collect tree ring cores have remade our understanding of the deep history of the Colorado River's flow.

It's also my own story. I was excited as a boy by stories of Powell's great adventure. That turned to excitement as an adult about Powell's great scientific adventure and the adventures of those who followed him.

I will never forget standing deep in the Grand Canyon, at the junction of the Colorado and Little Colorado rivers. It's the same place Powell was when he wrote: "We are three quarters of a mile in the depths of the earth, and the great river shrinks into insignificance as it dashes its angry waves against the walls and cliffs that rise to the world above; the waves are but puny ripples, and we but pigmies, running up and down the sands and lost among the boulders."

I felt the same way—humbled by the power of nature around me and curious to understand it better.

Acknowledgments

One of the great joys of my work is the generosity of the many scientists who so patiently explain their research to me. They are far too numerous to mention here, but special thanks for help in the preparation of this book goes to the staff of the Laboratory of Tree Ring Research at the University of Arizona, to Julio Betancourt, Henri Grissino-Mayer, Maya Elrick, Ken Drozd, Deirdre Kann, Connie Woodhouse, Tom Pagano, and Julie Cole.

Rapids on the Colorado River nearly ended John Wesley Powell's first trip through the Grand Canyon.

CHAPTER ONE

John Wesley Powell

Explorer and Scientist

John Wesley Powell pulled his boat, the *Emma Dean*, to the Colorado River's shore to scout the water ahead. The river roared through the rocks, tumbling over a fierce rapid. The 35-year-old former army major thought it would be better to carry the boats around the danger. But one of the boatmen behind him, O. G. Howland, didn't see the signal to land. Howland's boat, the *No Name*, shot into the rapids, out of control. Howland made it safely over the first rapids, a drop of 10 feet (three meters). Below, danger waited: a 50-foot (15-meter) drop "in a channel filled with dangerous rocks that broke the waves into whirlpools and beat them into foam," Powell wrote. The *No Name* slammed into a rock, throwing Howland, his brother, Seneca, and Frank Goodman into the muddy, swirling water. The three grabbed hold, but the boat was full of water. They could no longer steer it, and the boat crashed into another rock, splitting to pieces. Goodman and the Howland brothers were thrown into the river and washed around a bend, out of Powell's sight.

As he raced down the bank, Powell saw Goodman clinging for his life to a rock. A whirlpool raged around Goodman. O. G. Howland inched toward him with a long pole. Goodman let go of the rock and grabbed the pole, and Howland pulled him to safety. Seneca Howland found safety on an island farther downstream. The men were saved. But the *No Name*, and her precious cargo, seemed lost.

John Wesley Powell led a party of four boats and 10 men that summer of 1869. They hoped to be the first through "the Great Unknown"—a region Powell would later name the Grand Canyon of the Colorado River. Powell

Powell and his crew used simple wooden boats for their first trip down the Colorado River.

John F. Steward, a member of Powell's exploring party.

Calm water gave Powell and his crew a rest from the rapids. The picture is in two pieces because it is a stereograph, a three-dimensional image.

wanted to fill in the last blank spot on the map of the United States. He had been a major in the US Army during the Civil War. The members of his party were Civil War veterans and mountain men who had come west after the great battles, which had ended four years before. Their trip through the Grand Canyon was a daring adventure, and through newspaper accounts, the nation watched eagerly. But the trip had a serious scientific purpose—Powell wanted to use the tools of science to understand this land.

The canyon country of the western United States spans what we now call the Four Corners—Colorado, Utah, New Mexico, and Arizona. It was the last unknown on the maps of the young nation. Meriwether Lewis and William Clark had explored the Mississippi, Missouri, and Columbia rivers more than 60 years before. The deserts of the Four Corners proved far more forbidding to the European immigrants who were spreading across North America.

Native Americans had lived in the region for thousands of years and had mastered life in the *arid* land. But the European immigrants trying to make this continent their own came from wet places, where rivers flowed high and enough rain fell from the sky to water whatever crops they wanted to plant. They didn't understand how to live in a place this dry. Powell's mission was to use science to explain it to them.

Powell's map of the Grand Canyon was the first ever made of the unexplored region.

John Wesley Powell was the son of a Methodist minister, and his parents expected him to follow in his father's footsteps. But he had other ideas. In the 1860 census, Powell identified himself as a "naturalist." In those days, scientific education was more haphazard, and the young Powell was largely self-taught. But it was enough to land him a job as a schoolteacher until war got in the way.

Like many young American men of his time, John Wesley Powell fought in the Civil War. Captain Powell commanded Battery F of the

Second Light Artillery, Illinois Volunteers, at the horrible battle of Shiloh. Amid bitter fighting, Powell pointed one of his battery's cannons at a fence where Confederate soldiers were hiding. "As I raised my hand for a signal to the gunners to stand clear of the recoil," he wrote later, "a musket ball struck my arm above the wrist." In the raging battle, he scarcely noticed the wound. But within days, an army doctor had no choice but to amputate Powell's arm.

Powell wasn't the only young man whose life was changed forever at Shiloh. "Twenty thousand had been killed or wounded that day," wrote historian Donald Worster, "one of the deadliest battles in the annals of modern warfare." Despite his injury, Powell returned to battle.

When the war ended, Powell applied for a disability pension since he could do no physical labor. But his mind had always been his strength, and he soon landed a job as a professor at Illinois Wesleyan University. He had no actual college degree, just an honorary one given to him while he was in the army. But it was enough to launch the career of a man who would become one of America's great 19th-century scientists.

Camped beside the Colorado River, Powell couldn't sleep the night the *No Name* was lost. A quarter of the expedition's food was gone, but Powell had lost something far more important. In packing, he had carefully distributed the food and equipment equally among the four boats. That way, if one boat wrecked, the crew wouldn't be without anything they really needed. "But, in the distribution, there was one exception to this precaution," Powell wrote. "The barometers were all placed in one boat, and they are lost!" Powell used the *barometers*, instruments that measure air pressure, to measure the weather and to make maps. As you go up in elevation, the air gets thinner, which is why you breathe harder when hiking on top of a mountain—there's less air. Powell used the barometers to measure the heights of cliffs and the distance the river dropped as the explorers descended through its canyons, and he feared his hopes of making a good map were dashed in the wreck of the *No Name*.

The next morning, after breakfast, Powell scouted the site of the wreck. He spotted the cabin of the shattered boat, lodged in the middle of the river. Satisfied that his men could reach it safely, he dispatched a boat to get it.

> Sumner and Dunn volunteer to take the little boat and make the attempt. They start, reach it, and out come the barometers! The boys set up a shout, and I join them, pleased that they should be as glad as myself to save the instruments. When the boat lands on our side, I find that the only things saved from the wreck were the barometers, a package of thermometers, and a three-gallon keg of whiskey. The last is what the men were shouting about.

Powell's first trip through the Grand Canyon ended in both triumph and tragedy. Two days before the trip was over, three of Powell's men left the expedition. Afraid of a looming rapid, they decided to hike out of the treacherous canyon. They were never seen again.

Powell emerged from the canyon a national hero. But it wasn't enough to have simply run the river. Powell used his newfound reputation as a daring adventurer to persuade the US government to pay him to complete a serious scientific survey of the region. Thus began his transformation from explorer to scientist.

Two years later, Powell led a second group of explorers into the Canyon of Lodore, where the *No Name* had wrecked. The group found a sack of flour left behind two years before. "Andy baked biscuits for dinner out of the flour," expedition photographer Jack Hillers wrote in his diary. "Found it in perfect condition with the exception of a crust of an inch thick on the outside of the flour." More notable than the food, though, was the water in the river. It was lower this time through the canyon than when Powell had first explored it two years before.

The Greenhouse Effect

Without the earth's natural greenhouse effect, our planet would be unlivable. A delicate balance in the atmosphere has created a climate over the last 10,000 years that has made our lives possible. But humans are now tinkering with the atmosphere, with possibly dangerous results.

Sunlight provides the fuel for global weather cycles. But it's the atmosphere that determines how that weather plays out. When sunlight streams down through the atmosphere, most of it passes right through the air until it hits the earth. The air is transparent to the visible light emitted by the sun, which is why you can see through air.

Put your hand on black pavement on a hot summer day—it's very hot because the pavement absorbs sunlight. Now hold your hand a little above the pavement.

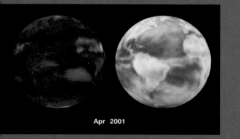

Apr 2001

This NASA satellite image show what happens when energy from the sun hits the Earth. On the right, you can see a small amount of sunlight reflected back into space. Most of the heat, left, heats the ground. The warm ground then emits a different kind of light called "infrared radiation," which is why the image on the left looks bright red. As greenhouse gases build up in the atmosphere, more of that infrared radiation is trapped in the lower atmosphere, leading to global warming.

Powell was beginning to understand why:

> This high region . . . is set with ranges of snow-clad mountains . . . All winter long snow falls on its mountain-crested rim, filling the gorges, half burying the forests, and covering the crags and peaks with a mantle woven by the winds from the waves of the sea. When the summer sun comes this snow melts and tumbles down the mountain sides in millions of cascades.

Some years, he was learning, more snow falls than others.

Powell's second trip down the Colorado was slower and more careful. The first time had been an adventure. Determined to make a reliable map, Powell allotted two years for the second trip. At the end of the first half of the journey, he and his crew stashed their boats at Lee's Ferry, at the mouth of the Pariah River, and spent the winter in the frontier settlement of Kanab, Utah.

When they resumed their trip the following spring, they faced a very different Colorado River. In 1871, they had an easy time of the rapids. The river of 1872 was a torrent, higher and more violent than anything Powell had yet seen in his few years there.

"The stream was thick with red mud, the condition from which it derived its name," wrote Frederick Dellenbaugh, a member of Powell's party, "and it swept along with a splendid vigour that betokened a large reserve flood in the high mountains." The party braved the rapids, despite fears from the settlers at Lee's Ferry that they faced death as they entered the Grand Canyon.

With harrowing rapids but high, fast water, the travelers made good time. But when they reached the mouth of the Kanab River, 143 miles (230 kilometers) downriver from Lee's Ferry, Powell decided it was too dangerous to go on. He feared they would never make it safely past Separation Rapids. "Well, boys," he said, "our voyage is done." Their hike out to Kanab marked the end of John Wesley Powell's career as a Colorado River runner.

It would be left to scientists a century later to explain what happened. Why was the river so low in 1871 that it was easy to run the rapids and so high in 1872 that Powell and his crew feared death?

Water managers in the United States measure a river's flow in cubic feet of water per second—cfs. When I stepped into an aluminum frame pontoon boat in the fall of 1997 with a group of scientists following in Powell's footsteps, the flow at Lee's Ferry was a steady and predictable 20,000 cfs (566 cubic meters per second). The river would rise a few thousand cfs every afternoon as the managers of the massive Glen Canyon Dam, 15 miles (24 kilometers) upstream, released water to generate electricity for air conditioners in Phoenix. It was a stable, predictable, modest flow.

There was no dam in Powell's day, nothing to hold back the melting snow. Modern science allows an educated guess about the flows as Powell and his crew set off from Lee's Ferry. In 1869, as Powell successfully ran

You can still feel the heat. When an object, like the black pavement, gets hot, it emits a different type of light called infrared. Your eye can't see it, but any hot object emits it.

That is how the earth's temperature stays in balance. Energy comes in from the sun, primarily in the form of visible light. The earth's surface heats up and emits infrared light that heads back out into space. When the incoming energy and the outgoing energy are the same, the earth's temperature is stable. But some gases in the air, like carbon dioxide, trap some of that infrared light, keeping it from heading back into space.

Carbon dioxide, a gas always present in the air, traps heat. As long as the amount of carbon dioxide doesn't change, it won't change the earth's temperature. But if you start adding carbon dioxide to the air, it starts trapping more heat, raising the earth's temperature, in the same way you get warmer if you add another blanket to your bed. It acts something like the glass in a greenhouse, which traps heat and allows people to grow plants in the winter.

When we burn gasoline or coal to fuel our cars or generate electricity, the exhaust contains carbon dioxide. Over the last several hundred years, the amount of carbon dioxide in the air has gone up a lot, and our planet has warmed up as a result. Scientists know the earth's climate has changed greatly in the past. But they worry that changes caused by our current greenhouse gas emissions could cause climate changes that drive some species of plants and animals to extinction. Some people could starve because of droughts caused by global warming or see their cities washed away by rising sea levels as the earth's ice melts.

Powell strapped a chair to his boat so he could sit higher to see rapids ahead.

the canyon, it was flowing at perhaps 10,000 cfs (283 cubic meters per second). Estimates based on modern studies suggest it may have been three times as full when he and his crew abandoned the river at Kanab.

Powell's band of explorers turned into a full-fledged government scienti-fic survey in the years that followed their hike out to Kanab. Their report to the US Congress in 1879, just seven years after they left the river, remains one of the most important scientific documents about the West ever published.

Powell called it *The Report on the Lands of the Arid Region*. He collected the most complete set of rainfall data for the country that was available in those early days and tried to explain what it meant. Traveling from east to west, the country gets drier, and farming gets harder. Beyond the 100th meridian—a line stretching from North Dakota through Texas—less than 20 inches (50 centimeters) of rain falls a year. Without irrigation—without building dams and ditches to get water to crops—agriculture was impossible west of the 100th meridian, Powell wrote.

But Powell noticed something more. The problem wasn't just that the West was dry.

One of his team, geologist G. K. Gilbert, spent time in Utah, studying the Great Salt Lake. The lake has no outlet, and so the only way water leaves is by *evaporation*, leaving its minerals behind. When the weather is

River rafters today use very
different boats to run the Grand Canyon.

wetter, the lake's level rises. When it's dry, the level falls.

Gilbert gathered stories from the Mormon settlers who had lived around the lake for decades. For years at a time, he found, the lake would rise. Then for years at a time, the lake would drop. Gilbert had found the first evidence for the years-long wet spells and dry periods that would shape the lives of the European immigrants trying to make a life in the arid land.

The limit of agriculture might be 20 inches (50 centimeters) of rain a year, Powell wrote in his report to Congress. "Many droughts will occur," he wrote. "Many seasons in a long series will be fruitless." It's a message Westerners still struggle to understand.

CHAPTER ONE **ACTIVITY**

The Journal

One of John Wesley Powell's most important accomplishments as he explored the Colorado River was to write down what he saw. He kept a journal, recording the data he collected and the experiences he and his men had. Today, his Colorado River journals are kept in the Smithsonian Institution in Washington, D.C. They are a valuable scientific record and a national treasure.

A scientist's most important tool is a field notebook. Scientists use their field notebook to record the information they collect while they are out working in the field. They write down what they saw and when they saw it, what they measured and where.

You will need the following tools for your field observations:

1. A notebook. It should be sturdy, with a solid back, because you may not be sitting at a desk when you write in it. The pages should turn easily.

2. A pen or pencil. Colored pencils are useful for drawing graphs.

You can use this notebook to record the data you collect doing the activities in this book. You can also use it to record daily observations on the weather. In later chapters, this book will show you how to set up scientific tools like thermometers and *rain gauges* to gather data on the weather and climate. But not all the data you collect requires equipment. For some observations, all you need is your senses.

Every day, write down the date and what the weather is like:

Is it cloudy? Sunny? Rainy? Foggy? Hot? Cold? Windy? Was there frost on the grass or on the car in front of your house? Does it seem warmer or colder than yesterday? Did the weather affect something you did? Was it a nice warm day to spend outside? So cold you had to come in to stay warm? Has it been so dry recently that your yard needed extra water? So wet that you have to wipe the mud off your shoes before you come inside?

Instruments to record weather data, like barometers, thermometers, and rain gauges, are important tools, and later you'll see how to use them. But information as simple as daily descriptions of weather, recorded over the centuries, has helped scientists learn about climate when more detailed data weren't available.

In the 1700s, before the widespread use of thermometers, local government officials in the Yangtze region of China made the *Qing Yu Lu*, the *Clear and Rain Records*. Every day, local officials wrote down whether it was clear, cloudy, foggy, or rainy. If it rained, they wrote down the time the rain started and ended. Modern scientists have turned to the *Qing Yu Lu* and other records like them from around the world to determine what ancient climates were like.

A sample field notebook page.

CHAPTER TWO

The Forecast

Ken Drozd stared at one of the five computer screens that surround the forecast desk at the Albuquerque office of the National Weather Service. The picture of the earth, taken by a satellite orbiting high overhead, showed a storm coming. Drozd's job is to figure out where and when it will hit.

Drozd is a *meteorologist*. As he drove to work just after sunup, he could see clear skies. But his job isn't to describe what the weather is like today—it's to figure out what it will be like tomorrow.

Drozd is one of the army of people behind the weather forecasts you see in the newspaper or hear on the radio and television. Weather forecasting may be the most high-profile science today. Every day, meteorologists collect all the weather data available to them and try to predict what will happen next. Drozd was fascinated

Ken Drozd collects computer data to help with his daily forecast.

with weather at an early age. He grew up in Nebraska, on the vast, flat expanse of the United States known as the Great Plains. As a child, he used to watch great thunderstorms roll in across the plains, pressing his nose against the screen door of his house. He was in high school when he decided to pursue meteorology as a career, taking a lot of math and science classes and earning a degree in meteorology at the University of Nebraska at Lincoln.

Outside Drozd's office, an electronic weather station delivers up-to-the-minute data on the wind and temperature. But to forecast the weather, you need much more than that.

First stop: satellites. Orbiting 22,190 miles (35,790 kilometers) above the earth, the GOES—Geostationary Operational Environmental Satellites—send down a stream of pictures and data about the world below. The pictures that day showed clouds as a storm swept across the central Pacific Ocean. They showed water vapor—essentially wet air—seeping into the western United States. From west to east across the Northern *Hemisphere*, Drozd's satellite pictures showed storms marching across the planet. Equally important were the gaps between the storms—those are the places where the weather is dry.

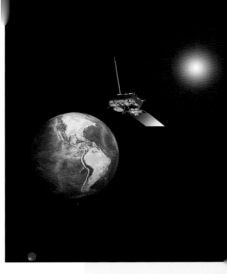

Satellites help meteorologists observe weather on the earth.

What we think of as "the weather" happens where we live, at the earth's surface. But the atmosphere above us is complex and what matters to Drozd as he works out the details of the day's forecast happens far above him.

The earth's atmosphere extends hundreds of miles above the planet's surface, but most of what influences our weather happens in the first six miles (10 kilometers)—a layer called the *troposphere*.

On this particular day, Albuquerque sat in a gap between two storms. But to the northwest, over Idaho, Drozd could see a storm forming. On his computer map, it looked like a big blob of gray, with colored bits in the center where the clouds were the largest. His job was to figure out when that storm would hit New Mexico.

Seen from space, weather swirls around our planet.

Looking at the satellite maps can be trickier than it seems. Looking down from above, the satellite sees clouds as areas of white. But places where snow is on the ground look white too. To tell the difference, Drozd played a sort of movie made of multiple satellite images taken over the previous 12 hours. The clouds moved. The snow didn't.

Maxine Pacheco launches a weather balloon. The small box tethered beneath the balloon radios back data as it rises into a storm, telling forecasters about the temperature, humidity, and wind high in the atmosphere.

Next stop: the *sounding*. Every 12 hours, a weather balloon is launched from a little brick building behind the National Weather Service Forecast Office, carrying a package of instruments called a *radiosonde*. As it flies up into the atmosphere, it radios back data about what it sees: the temperature, the humidity, and the winds. A chart on Drozd's computer showed what the most recent balloon launch found.

The squiggles on the resulting weather balloon chart show Drozd what is going on in the sky above him. Is the air above warm or cool, wet or dry? Which way is the wind blowing? All across the United States—around the world, in fact—weather balloons are launched every 12 hours. All of that information is available to Drozd, providing the critical variables to include as he thinks about what will happen next with the weather.

But the most important tool is found on the computer itself: the *forecast model*. Every six hours, a supercomputer in Maryland grinds out a massive calculation to estimate what the weather will be like for the next two weeks all over the world. Data from every weather balloon launched around the world are fed into the computer. Data from weather stations are added to the mix, along with satellite images.

The results are a prediction of the future. On his computer, Drozd can click hour by hour to see what the computer thinks the weather will be like. What track does the computer think the storm will follow? What temperature does the computer think New Mexico will be when the storm gets there? But Drozd has been at the weather-forecasting business long enough to know that he can't trust the computer completely. Its predictions can be off by a bit. His job is to use his judgment, developed over years of experience, and refine the message that is delivered to the public with his midday forecast.

A computer map helps meteorologists forecast the weather.

Computer forecasts are good, and they continue to improve, Drozd explains. But the human element—combining scientific knowledge with intuition, the ability to recognize patterns and knowledge of the local landscape—can make forecasts that are even better.

Water Vapor

It's no exaggeration to say that no one knows water vapor quite the way Mel Strong does.

The traces of water in air are critical for making weather. The vapor starts as water in lakes, as the ocean, or as moisture in plants or the soil on land. Occasionally, as the water *molecules* bounce around in the liquid, one molecule has enough energy to break free and make it up into the air. The warmer the water, the more energy the molecules have and the easier it is for one to break free. That is called *evaporation*. When the water evaporates, it turns into a gas that is invisible. When that vapor condenses, it makes fog, rain, or snow. Storms are driven in part by the amount of moisture in the air.

In the summer, that is especially important in the southwestern United States. Moist air billows up into the atmosphere, creating great thunderstorms. But the question of where all that moisture comes from has long been a mystery. Unlike the great clouds that make up winter storms, the water vapor that eventually turns into thunderstorms is invisible. It drifts this way and that, and by the time it makes it into a thunderstorm, no one is quite sure where it came from.

That is the task Strong tackled as a Univer-sity of New Mexico *graduate student*. Every day, Strong goes up to the roof of the university's geology department building in the heart of Albuquerque and collects a sample of air. Downstairs in the lab, he painstakingly extracts the traces of water vapor contained in the air and studies them for clues about where the water came from.

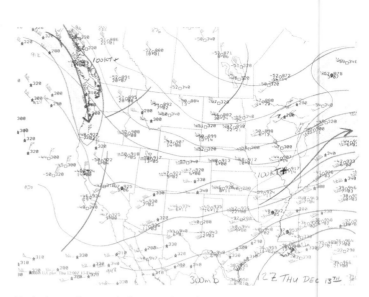

To help understand the weather, forecasters sometimes also draw maps by hand.

To go beyond computer forecasts, Drozd and his colleagues often, surprisingly, do forecasting work by hand. On his desk is a paper printout of the current weather conditions. On the printout, Drozd has used colored pencils to draw in the *jet stream*, the river of high-altitude air flowing from west to east that shepherds storms across North America. In winter in New Mexico, the position of the jet stream is critical to forecasting the next storm. In general, the jet stream moves large weather systems from west to east. But the jet stream doesn't move in a straight line. It whips north and south, twisting and buckling like a garden hose turned on full blast with no one to hold it in place.

To understand where the jet stream is and what it might do next, Drozd goes beyond the computer, pulling out a pencil and working out the details for himself to make sure he understands what is going on.

We think of the weather in terms of the air around us at the earth's surface. But to understand what happens there, meteorologists like Drozd need to understand conditions all through the atmosphere, from ground level to high above the earth.

In the layer that matters, the troposphere, air is always moving. The most important thing driving it is the sun, which blankets half of the earth at a time in warmth. The resulting air movement is all driven by that energetic solar bath. The key to understanding why the air is always moving so much—why, for example, that storm in Idaho is bearing down on New Mexico as Drozd works over his daily forecast—involves the difference between the heat at the earth's *equator* and the poles.

Heat tends to move from hot places toward cold places. You can think of this in the opposite way, too. Cold wants to move toward warm places. Open your refrigerator and you can feel the cold air coming out. If you lived in the refrigerator, you would feel the warm air coming in.

That is exactly what happens, on a very large scale, on the earth. The sun beating down on the earth's midsection, the equator, heats things up there. The North and South poles, meanwhile, are very cold, because they get so much less sunlight. Like your kitchen when the refrigerator door is open, the earth is constantly experiencing a flow of warmth from the equator toward the poles. Meteorologists call this a giant *heat engine* that drives the earth's weather.

Another way of looking at air movement, Drozd said, is that air is always trying to achieve a state of

Mel Strong flies high to collect water vapor samples.

But collecting water from the roof of the building isn't enough. What if the water vapor in the air high above the ground is different? So every so often, Strong takes to the air in what he calls his "flying machine." It's a small aircraft called an *ultralight*. It looks like a cross between a parachute and a glider, with a motor to drive it. Strong flies slowly up into the air above central New Mexico, collecting air samples as he goes, to determine the differences in the water vapor found at different altitudes, or heights, above the ground.

His goal is to understand the source of the water vapor that eventually gives rise to New Mexico's summer thunderstorms. Does it come from the Pacific Ocean? The Gulf of California? The Gulf of Mexico? Strong and the other scientists he's working with hope the answers they find contribute to our understanding of the droughts that so often cause so many problems in the Southwest.

equilibrium and equal balance. This is true of both temperature and pressure. Air essentially flows from *high pressure* to *low pressure*, like it does when you let air out of a balloon or how water flows downhill.

The clear air above him as Drozd arrived at work is the result of high-pressure air over New Mexico. High pressure is usually associated with sinking air that leads to clear skies. To the northwest, an area of low pressure sat over Idaho. The jet stream is pointed from Idaho straight toward New Mexico. Over the next 24 hours, Drozd thinks the storm will move down across the western United States, bringing rain and snow to New Mexico.

Seeing the storm coming is easy. Figuring out exactly where it will end up is harder. The computer model shows it dipping into northwest New Mexico and then swinging to the east, across the state's northern mountains, before it exits across the Great Plains. The question is how far south it will get.

This matters a lot to Drozd, because he knows he's writing a forecast for people, and the largest audience is the big city of Albuquerque, in the center of New Mexico. The question is how wet Albuquerque will become.

Forecasters answer questions like that probabilistically, meaning they often can't say for sure what will happen. Remember that the jet stream is like a whipping garden hose turned on full blast. Exactly how far it will whip, and in which direction, is hard to predict exactly.

Drozd knows there is a chance the storm will hit Albuquerque, but not much of a chance. On the computer forecast map he is building, he sets the number at 20 percent. He moves up to the cities of Taos and Farmington, taking the computer model's guidance and his own experience of storms like this and making his best estimate for each of the main cities in New Mexico where people live.

Then comes the trickiest part of all. People hoping to drive the next day want to know whether they will experience rain or snow. In areas where it's very cold, this is an easy call: snow. In warm areas, Drozd's forecast calls for rain. The tricky part is the line between the two. Painstakingly,

Snow and storms spread across the western United States, as seen from space.

Drozd goes over the forecast maps showing him how warm the computer thinks it will be the next day across the forecast area. He looks not only at surface temperatures, but the forecast for the air high above the ground. If conditions are right, a very dangerous thing can happen: precipitation can start falling as rain, then hit the ground and freeze. Ice storms are one of the most dangerous weather phenomena possible. Drozd is on the lookout for chances that might happen so he can issue a warning to drivers to stay off the roads.

His work done, Drozd clicks the mouse to send his forecast to the National Weather Service's computers so it can be distributed to the public—over the radio, on television, in the newspaper, and on the web. And he immediately starts looking ahead to see what is coming next, getting ready for another day's forecast.

"We keep learning all the time," he says.

Observing the Weather

On December 4, 1890, archaeologist Adolph Bandelier wrote in his diary:

> It seems that there is going to be a big snowfall. It is a blessing for the garden. It continued thus, threatening with snow and cold all day, but nothing happened.

Thermometer.

One of the keys to understanding weather and climate is collecting data about it every single day. Your observations about what weather looks and feels like are important. But for about the last century, modern weather record keepers have done more, recording detailed data about conditions. Weather stations usually record the daytime high temperature, the overnight low temperature, and how much rain or snow fell, along with their observations about how sunny or cloudy the weather was.

You will need:

1. A thermometer

2. Your notebook

You can find an inexpensive thermometer at any garden store. Some are specially designed to register the high and low temperature every day. That will help, but it's not required for this project.

Find a shady spot outside for your thermometer. Official weather stations use a shelter to protect the thermometer from the sun, but for this project, tacking it up on the side of a tree is fine. One of the thermometers at my house is under the shade of the front porch. That's not the best spot because the porch keeps it warm at night, but it's easy to see out the front window without having to go outside on cold mornings.

If you have a *maximum-minimum thermometer*, write down the high temperature and low temperature it registers every day. If you have a regular thermometer, read it twice a day—once around breakfast time and once in the late afternoon, right before dinner. Also note any other weather events that happen. Did it rain? Did it snow? Was it cloudy when you took your reading? Was it sunny?

After you have collected data for a week, look at the data to see if patterns are starting to develop. Is it cooler or warmer on cloudy days? On cloudy mornings, is it warmer or colder? Why do you think that might be?

Back in December 1890, Adolph Bandelier noted in his diary that after threatening for a day, the snow finally came:

> Snow and snow; night and day without cease. What favorable weather!

CHAPTER THREE

Maya Elrick

Student of Ancient Climates

Geologist Maya Elrick measures layers of rock to understand ancient climates.

Maya Elrick stood high on a steep mountain face in the Bridger Mountains of western Montana. The work was tedious. Every inch or so, she leaned hard against her battery-powered drill. The drill was made to bite into brick, not do science, but scientists have to improvise. With each turn of the drill, Elrick drove out a tiny cascade of dust and caught it in an envelope. She sealed each envelope for the trip back to her Virginia lab.

The rocks were laid out in neat layers, each a few inches thick, stretching up the cliff like an endless layer cake with no frosting. The neatness amazed Elrick—an orderly repeating pattern of thick dark layers and thin light ones. "I had to ask," she says, "what caused this?"

Weather and *climate* are two different things, but it's easy to get them confused. Understanding the difference helps explain the question Elrick confronted on that Montana cliff.

Weather is what happens day to day. One day it rains, and the next day is sunny and dry. One day is hot, and the next one is cold. Each day can be very different from the day before, but over a few years or decades, a pattern emerges. In deserts, there are more dry days. Jungles have more wet days. In the Sahara desert in

Africa, most days are hot; in Antarctica, most days are cold. The pattern that emerges over time, the long-term average, is called climate.

That seems a simple enough way to think about the difference between weather and climate. Over the span of a human lifetime, climate doesn't change much. Deserts stay deserts, and jungles stay jungles. For most of what we humans do, understanding the climate of the recent past is enough. But over thousands or millions of years, climate changes. The earth as a whole can get hotter or colder, or the climate over large areas can get wetter or drier. Five thousand years ago, much of what is now the hot, dry Sahara was green and wet. If the climate changes happen quickly enough, they can affect human societies. A drought just 10 years long can doom a community that is unprepared. Plants, animals, and people can be forced to move or can die.

Today, vast networks of thermometers, *rain gauges*, and other scientific instruments circle the globe. Satellites looking down from space measure sea level and rainfall, which is how we know what is happening with our weather and climate. But what if we want to know what climate was like long ago?

Thermometers and rain gauges have been on the earth for a few centuries at most—far less in most places. Scientists like Elrick, studying *paleoclimate*, have to be clever to find the traces left behind by a changing climate. Elrick knew that the layers extending up the cliff in the Bridger Mountains might be one such clue.

Elrick slowly inched up the rock face, drilling as she went. To a geologist like Elrick, tens of thousands of years is the blink of an eye. Three hundred and fifty million years ago, the rocks that now make up this high mountain cliff were deposited as mud at the bottom of a shallow sea. Elrick was looking for evidence of what the climate was like then.

The rocks, called *sedimentary* rocks, are formed layer by layer as silt and dead sea creatures settle on the ocean floor. Over time, as they are buried, heat and pressure change them from ocean bottom muck to solid rock. Then, as the earth's continents slowly move around the planet,

Muddy rivers leave climate clues in the sediments they carry to the sea.

crashing together and drifting apart, mountains like the Bridgers can be pushed high into the sky. To finish off the picture, about 10,000 years ago a *glacier* carved away the cliff face Elrick was working on, exposing the rocks and allowing scientists like her to go to work.

Studying ancient rocks might seem a strange way to study the earth's climate. What do rocks have to do with rain and snow, warm days and cold? The answer is that climate leaves its fingerprints in the rocks. Elrick, a 28-year-old graduate student, climbed the steep mountain back in the summer of 1988 to read them.

When I was talking to Elrick in her office at the University of New Mexico, in Albuquerque, it was the start of the desert's summer rainy season. To explain how the rocks in her study were formed, she pointed out the window toward the Rio Grande, a few miles to the west. Heavy thunderstorms wash dirt into the river, turning it a thick, muddy brown. That, she said, was how some of the rocks she was studying were made. As the Rio Grande flows toward the Gulf of Mexico after a heavy storm, it carries that dirt with it full of heavy sand particles, leaving a layer on the ocean floor—evidence of the flood that just happened.

Now imagine the Rio Grande during the dry season. It still flows, but it wanders lazily to the Gulf of Mexico. It still looks dirty, but only fine silt can be carried because the water isn't moving quickly enough to carry the heavier sand grains. The layer it leaves behind on the ocean floor will be made of fine silt, like the dust on your windowsill.

The same thing can happen on a larger scale during the spring runoff season. Snow falls all winter in the mountains. In the spring, it melts and flows out to sea. If there is a lot of snow, the runoff is heavy, and it can carry heavy sand grains. The layer that ends up at the sea, at the river's mouth, is made up of those heavy sand grains. If there is little snow, the runoff is light, and the only thing that makes it to the sea is fine silt. That's how the layer of muck building up in the ocean at the river's edge records climate far inland, where the river takes shape.

The layers Elrick now studies took many hundreds of years to build up as muck on the ocean floor. They are a record of climate conditions 350 million years ago.

Day after day, Elrick hiked up the cliff to measure a steep section a thousand feet high. The rocks were in layers—thick, thin, thick, thin and told a story about a climate that had been wet, dry, wet, dry. But to complete the story, Elrick needed to know precisely how thick each layer was. That would tell her how long it took each layer to form.

Geology sounds like fun, and it is. For weeks at a time, Elrick camped in the high country. She climbed some of the most beautiful mountains of the West, doing for her job what other people do on their vacations.

But geology is also hard, tedious work. To get samples of rock, Elrick used a power drill. There are no electric outlets on the side of a mountain,

Layered rocks carried back from the field provide laboratory clues.

Maya Elrick.

so she went to a hardware store and bought a drill—the kind you would use to work on your house—with a rechargeable battery so she could use it on the mountainside. But because there were no electrical outlets at the campground to recharge the drill, every night, after a long day in the field, she drove down the mountain to the Bridger Bowl Ski Area. The ski area was closed for the summer, but she found an outdoor electrical outlet. She sat and read while the batteries charged.

Back at her Virginia Tech lab, Elrick spent weeks analyzing the samples she had drilled out of the mountainside, testing each sample to see how much of it was silt and how much of it was sand—how much had been made in a dry climate and how much in a wet climate.

The earth's weather starts with sunlight. That provides the energy that drives the system. Sunlight's warmth evaporates the water that becomes rain, and its energy pushes and pulls the winds that move storms around the planet's surface. Change the amount of sunlight hitting the earth and the climate changes. You experience this every year in our most obvious climate cycle—the seasons. The earth is tilted on its rotating axis. The half of the planet tilted toward the sun gets more light, which is why summer is hot. The half tilted away from the sun experiences winter, which is why Australians, living on the southern half of the planet, can celebrate Christmas on a warm, sunny summer day at the beach.

The differences in the seasons cause obvious yearly climate patterns. But Elrick's data showed something happening much more slowly, over far longer periods. By calculating the age of the entire section of rock and then dividing by the number of layers, she realized that the earth's climate 350 million years ago was switching from wet to dry and back again every few thousand years, like clockwork. These are the sort of changes that happen too slowly to be noticed in a person's lifetime. But in geologic terms, that's fast.

When Elrick first talked to me about her research many years ago, she told me about the work of Columbia University geologist Gerard Bond. Bond found evidence for similar cycles in sediments on the floor of the North Atlantic. Much like the layers in Elrick's ancient rocks, Bond's ocean floor sediments seem to show that modern climate has been changing every few thousand years.

That means cycles of climate change every few thousand years might not be unique to the modern age or to the period 350 million years ago, when Elrick's Bridger Mountain rocks formed.

For two decades, Elrick has studied rocks all over North America in search of the answer. She was looking for other places where the layers followed the same few-thousand-year rhythm. Again and again, she found them—from the tops of New Mexico mountains to the hills of western Canada. In 17 different places, she has found rocks with layers caused by climate change, repeating every few thousand years.

What causes the climate changes? The most likely explanation seems to be the sun. Tiny changes in the amount of energy from the sun hitting the earth could change the path that storms follow across the planet, like a railroad switch shunting a train from one track to another. Push the storm pathways away from an area and it will get drier. Bring the storm pathways closer to the same region and it will get wetter. Perhaps the sun itself has a pattern, getting slowly brighter and dimmer every few thousand years. Scientists today monitor the sun closely, but they haven't been doing it long enough to detect the sort of slow-moving changes it would take to cause the climate change patterns that Elrick found in the Bridger Mountain rocks. So the mystery remains.

Such is the way of science. Often, the new discoveries you make raise more questions than answers.

Elrick's office is full of rocks, brought back from around the world for study.

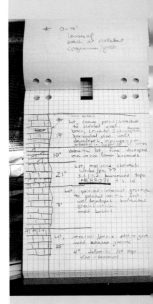

Meticulous field notes are critical to scientists.

Solving Scientific Puzzles

Scientists can't always look things up in a book. When they face a new question, they often have to invent a new way to answer it. That is the situation Maya Elrick faced in the Bridger Mountains. Drilling her way up the cliff, taking tiny samples of rock dust every few inches, was hard, tedious work. She knew that if she could find a faster, easier way, she would be able to study more mountains.

The idea was to identify the rock type all the way up the cliff as the layers changed. Drilling out samples and taking the dust back to the lab was a sure thing. But what if she could just look at the rock and tell what kind it was? If she could do that accurately, it would save a lot of time.

Elrick and her adviser, Fred Read, hit on an idea. What if she had a way to simply measure the rock as she went up the cliff face, unrolling a long strip of paper

Drywall tape, which you can buy at a hardware store, proved crucial to Elrick's field work.

CHAPTER THREE **ACTIVITY**

What Is "the Temperature"?

You hear it all the time: "The temperature today was 87 degrees." But what do we mean by "the temperature"?

Air is made up of tiny molecules, bouncing this way and that. The faster they move, the warmer the air is. The slower they move, the colder the air is. Air temperature is a measurement of their average speed.

But the air temperature can be very different in different places. Every 12 hours, professional weather observers launch balloons with thermometers attached to measure the temperature above the earth's surface. The higher the balloons go, the colder the air gets. But the temperature can change just a few feet above the ground. This activity will show the differences in those first few feet.

To make sure their data are reliable, scientists spend a lot of time trying to ensure the data are collected in a consistent way. For measuring air temperature, that means setting up all the thermometers in roughly the same way. The US National Weather Service's Cooperative Observer Program asks volunteers to take temperature readings every day. The program's guidelines call for the thermometer to be placed in an open area, five feet off the ground, away from buildings and pavement. The thermometer must be shaded from the sun.

You will need:

1. Two thermometers

2. Your field notebook

Find a fence post or wall, shaded from the sun. Attach one of the thermometers as close as you can to the ground without touching it and the second at about eye level.

When you take your daily temperature measurements, note the readings of both thermometers. How different are they? Which thermometer is warmer and which is colder in the early morning? Which thermometer is warmer and which is colder in the late afternoon? How do those results change on a cloudy day or a sunny day? How does it change if the air is still or windy?

Here's what is happening.

Sunlight doesn't warm the atmosphere directly. Instead, it streams straight through the air and stops when it hits a solid object, like the ground. The sunlight's energy heats the ground, and then the ground heats the air above it. The result is that during the day, the atmosphere heats from the bottom up.

At night, the opposite effect happens. The warmed earth cools off by radiating its energy back out toward space. As the earth cools, it cools the air closest to the ground first. If it's windy, that cool layer is quickly stirred up. If the air is still, the cool layer hugs the surface of the ground. That's why you can have a layer of frost on your lawn or frost on your car when your eye-level thermometer tells you "the temperature" is above freezing. The ground in that case has cooled the layer of air closest to it to below freezing while the air a few feet higher is too warm to register as freezing on your thermometer.

as she went and marking the different rock types? Could she eyeball it and get the markings right? Would they be as accurate as the precise data on rock type she got by dissolving the rock dust in acid in the lab?

Elrick employed a trick often used by scientists when they want to test out a new method. They use their old, tried-and-true method and the new one side by side. If they come out with the same answer, that means the new method works.

To make the markings, Elrick used ordinary drywall tape, which carpenters used to tape up the joints in wall boards when they are building a house. It's sturdy and a bit stiff but easy to roll and unroll. Most importantly, it's easy to write on.

After weeks in the lab, Elrick compared the results of her long strip of drywall tape and the samples she had drilled out of the rock. The answers she came up with—the width of the layers of rock—were the same. The next time out, she knew she wouldn't have to drill.

A thermometer placed near the ground will read differently than one at eye level because the temperature is different.

CHAPTER FOUR

A. E. Douglass

Founder of Tree Ring Science

Scientists wondered whether changes in climate could have caused the residents of what is now Bandelier National Monument to leave hundreds of years ago.

Northern New Mexico in the early 20th century was a dry place. But how long had it been that way? To scientists studying the ruins of ancient Native American cultures, this was a crucial question. Had northern New Mexico once been wetter? Did the residents of those ancient cities leave because the climate went from wet to dry?

That was the question posed by scientists poring over the ruins of an ancient community in what is now Bandelier National Monument, near Los Alamos, New Mexico. Residents lived and farmed in a wide spot in Frijoles Canyon, alongside a creek that ran year-round. Then, for some reason, they left, abandoning a prosperous city.

Two years of study by a team of scientists beginning in 1910 left more questions than answers. The scientists' best guess was that the climate got drier, forcing the people to leave. They had very little evidence. But in a 1913 report laying out their results, they offered a suggestion: "Any changes which may have occurred during the last few centuries," they wrote, "should be revealed by an extended study of the growth rings of coniferous trees. Many such trees in New Mexico and Arizona are from 300 to 500 years old, and some doubtless even older."

It was a simple suggestion, almost an afterthought. It included a footnote to some interesting new research by a scientist named A. E. Douglass. A few months before, Douglass had published a short paper in the journal *Science*: "A Method of Approximating Rainfall Over Long Periods and Some Results of Its Application."

Andrew Ellicott Douglass could not have intended to launch one scientific revolution, let alone two. He was just looking for a place in the woods of northern Arizona in the late 1800s to put a new telescope.

Douglass was an *astronomer*, not an *archaeologist*. Climate science barely existed at the time. But his side trip from astronomy into the study of tree rings changed both archaeology and climate science in ways that are still being felt.

To anyone who has looked at a cut tree, the rings radiating out from the center are obvious. The cut and polished log is a natural history museum staple. Little tags often identify the year Columbus sailed to the Americas and Washington crossed the Delaware. Tree ring science works because of the unique way trees grow. Each year, they put on a layer of new growth on the outside, between the tree's bark and its wood. The growing layer is called the *cambium*. As the tree's growth slows down for the winter, a thin layer of dark cells is added, creating a distinct light-dark pattern. The insight that turned those rings into a science was the realization that there was a story in the differences between fat and thin bands.

Douglass was born in Vermont in 1867, two years before John Wesley Powell made his first trip down the Grand Canyon. Douglass was a member of the last generation of scientists who could be successful studying a little of everything rather than specializing in one topic. He trained as an astronomer, but when

A. E. Douglass.

he went to Peru as a young man to set up a telescope, he also collected fossils and studied geology.

In a letter from Peru to his sister, he described an earthquake he and his colleagues lived through. "The shake is said to be a violent one, but if we don't get any better ones than that, I shall be disappointed." It wasn't just astronomy that excited him.

Douglass came to Arizona in 1894 looking for a place to build a telescope because Percival Lowell, a wealthy businessman and amateur astronomer, wanted to study Mars, and Lowell hired Douglass to supervise the project. The site he found was on a hill outside Flagstaff. For scientific history, it was a lucky choice. Flagstaff was a high-country town in the woods of northern Arizona. Douglass's main job may have been the study of Mars, but while he was in Flagstaff, he couldn't help noticing the trees.

When loggers cut down the big ponderosa pines—"yellow pines," they called them in those days—Douglass noticed the rings on the stumps or on the logs they hauled away.

Douglass's curiosity had little to do with climate. He was fascinated with the sun, the nearest star to the earth. Astronomers were beginning to realize that the sun's fires weren't constant but varied slightly over the years. Dark spots on the sun's surface called *sunspots* were the most obvious sign. Scientists who had tracked them discovered an 11-year cycle of increasing and decreasing sunspots. Douglass wondered whether that would affect the earth's weather. If it did, he thought, the patterns of variation might show up in the width of the trees' rings. That would allow him to use tree rings to go back in history, to before anyone had recorded sunspots, to see if the 11-year cycle was always there.

Douglass described what he was looking for in this way: "For centuries, these magnificent pines have stood there enduring all the vicissitudes of heat and cold, flood and drought. They should contain a record of such alterations."

In January 1904, Douglass went to the log yard at the Arizona Lumber and Timber Company. He wanted to test his idea. Slowly, he measured the width of rings on the end of a log. There was snow on the ground, and it was cold, hard work. But he seemed to be getting results, so Douglass persuaded the lumber company's president, T. A. Riordan, to have his workers cut five more thin sections off the end of logs and send them to him "in town, there to be measured more conveniently." Then Douglass went out into the woods and supervised the cutting of pieces out of 19 more trees so their rings could be measured.

He would place a steel ruler on the wood and, peering through a magnifying glass, he and his assistant would measure the width of each ring. By 1909, Douglass and his assistant had measured some 10,000 rings on 25 trees. To analyze what they found required thousands of calculations. Today's tree ring scientists feed their data into computers; Douglass and his assistant had to do it with pencil and paper. But their work was rewarded. The resulting patterns of fat and thin rings they found seemed to show an 11-year cycle, matching the pattern in the sunspot cycle they were looking for. The effect of the sunspots was tiny, though. It wasn't enough to use to predict the weather. But it was enough to convince Douglass he was on to something.

In the years that followed, Douglass perfected the techniques needed to use tree rings to estimate how much rain had fallen. "The radial thickness of the rings of the yellow pine of northern Arizona gives a measure of the rainfall in that vicinity with an average accuracy of over 70 percent," he wrote. But his most famous use of tree rings was in the study of archaeology. Scientists could cut pieces of timbers used to build the old Indian

Douglass realized the rings visible in the cross section of a tree could tell him about climate.

Scientists match up the patterns in tree rings from trees of many ages, looking for segments covering periods that overlap. When enough overlapping segments are found, the scientists can work their way back in time, identifying the years when the trees were cut down to build ancient human cities.

Scientists used tree rings to understand what the climate was like when people abandoned the ruins at what is now Bandelier National Monument in northern New Mexico.

ruins that dotted the West. Matching up the patterns of fat and thin rings, they were able to create a sort of calendar that allowed them to date when the tree had been cut and so when the structure it was used in was built.

Even more important, archaeologists were able to begin thinking about what sort of climate conditions the ancient Native Americans had experienced. The tree rings showed them that long-term droughts had often happened in the past and that they might have been part of the story of what caused the ancient civilizations to collapse.

In Bandelier National Monument, the questions posed by those scientists earlier in the 20th century were finally answered by tree rings. There had been no gradual drying trend at Bandelier as the early scientists had thought, but many short-term droughts. Eventually, the residents of Bandelier had moved down into the river valley below, which had a more reliable, permanent supply of water.

Tree rings.

Douglass realized the importance of what he was doing. "If the study works out as it promises," he said during a 1922 talk, "it will give a basis of long-range weather forecasting of immense practical value for the future and of large scientific value in interpreting the climate of the past."

The first part of that statement turned out to be wrong. Douglass and others hoped they could use tree rings and other weather data to detect predictable climate cycles. If you knew that every 23rd year was going to be dry, you could plan for it. Despite huge efforts, no scientist has been able to find predictable climate cycles. But for interpreting the climate of the past, Douglass's comment is an understatement. Tree rings have indeed had "large scientific value."

CHAPTER FOUR ACTIVITY

Measuring the Rain

Rain gauges are the simplest instruments in your backyard weather station but also the most important. They catch the rain from a storm, allowing you to measure it.

You will need:

1. A rain gauge

2. Your journal

Rain gauge.

You can buy an inexpensive rain gauge at a garden store or the garden department of a hardware store. They generally have a wide top that funnels to a narrow area marked with the measurements. That makes it easy to measure when just a small amount of rain falls.

When you make your daily thermometer check, write down in your journal how much rain fell since the last time you measured. Then empty the rain gauge so it will be ready for the next measurement. If no rain fell, write a 0. Sometimes you will know that it rained, but so little falls that you can't see any in the gauge. Meteorologists call that a "trace" of rain. Write *trace* in your journal.

Total up each month's rainfall.

In the United States, rain is usually measured in inches. In much of the rest of the world, rain is measured in millimeters, abbreviated mm. Scientists also use millimeters. Using two different systems for measurement can be confusing, so it's a good thing to learn to use both.

To convert from inches to millimeters, multiply the number of inches by 25.4:

0.5 inch = 12.7 mm

In your journal, record both numbers.

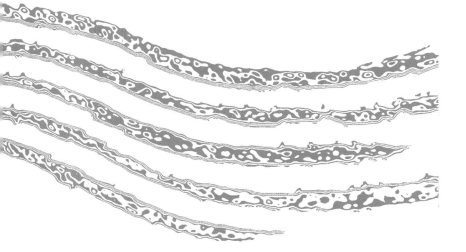

CHAPTER FIVE

Chaco Canyon

Climate, Trees, and the End of a Civilization

Julio Betancourt was just out of college, on a trip with friends, when he asked a question that would change his life. He was standing atop a cliff above Pueblo Bonito, an ancient ruin in Chaco Canyon. Chaco, in what is now northwestern New Mexico, was a vibrant city some 900 years ago. The ruins are stark and beautiful, and they evoke thoughts of the rich community that once lived here. But Betancourt wasn't thinking about people; he was thinking about trees. Or rather, he was thinking about the lack of trees.

The pueblos of Chaco Canyon were built in a high-elevation desert. In the hundred years scientists have had rain gauges there, it has averaged less than nine inches (23 centimeters) of precipitation a year. Not much can grow in a place that dry. But most of the high-elevation southwestern deserts Betancourt had visited were covered with piñon and juniper, tough, scrubby little trees that have carved out a niche in the high country of the desert Southwest. There were no trees at Chaco Canyon.

Betancourt and his friends climbed a trail up the cliff above Pueblo Bonito, the largest and most beautiful of the Chaco ruins. As they stood looking down, a large crow wheeled across the sky. Betancourt turned to his friends. "We're at 6,300 feet," he said. "This should be piñon-juniper woodland." The question of why it wasn't has occupied Betancourt's life ever since. It has taken him deep into the heart of climate science and helped us understand how these people lived here 900 years ago. It also may tell us something about one of science's great puzzles. Why did they leave?

Now desolate Chaco Canyon once was home to a thriving population. But scientist Julio Betancourt stood on this cliff and wondered, Why aren't there any trees?

Julio Betancourt is a great believer in doing science the way he did it that day on the cliff trail in Chaco Canyon—by looking around and thinking about what you see. "You do kind of rely on nature to tell you what's important and what's not," he says. He also is a believer in the value of scientific accidents, or serendipity. Scientific discoveries are often pretty serendipitous, he adds. But luck, as the saying goes, favors a prepared mind.

A big, friendly man with a beard, Julio Betancourt is the son of Cuban immigrants. He loves nothing more than to talk about his science. When you get him started, the conversation can quickly wander in directions no one intended. A conversation with Betancourt can range from the chemistry of grasses and how they respond to changes in climate to the vast patterns of ocean temperatures in the North Atlantic. He spent much of his career at the Desert Laboratory, on top of a small hill on the western edge of Tucson, Arizona. Big saguaro cacti dominate the landscape outside. Betancourt knows the arid western United States intimately. He works for the US Geological Survey—a government agency founded by John Wesley Powell to bring science into public service. But Betancourt's travels have taken him to the great Atacama Desert of South America and to arid Australia. Studying deserts has occupied his adult life.

Pack rat.

Betancourt's first great scientific accident was that question on the Chaco cliff. The second happened a few years later, when some friends taught him about a little rodent that lives in desert caves—*Neotoma*, the pack rat. Pack rats build small dens in caves, bringing back bits of plants that live nearby. Almost anything that happens to be growing in the neighborhood ends up in the pack rat's trash pile of a den. Scientists call these dens *middens*.

Since the caves are protected, a scientist coming around years later can tell what used to grow in the neighborhood. All they need is way of telling how old the midden is. *Carbon dating*, a technique for telling how long ago a plant or an animal died, provided the tool.

Sometimes, scientists get ideas at the strangest times. A scientist once explained to me how he came up with the solution to a problem while riding his bicycle to work. For Betancourt, it happened as he was walking around the duck pond at the University of New Mexico. He realized that pack rat middens could answer his Chaco question. He was so excited that he walked around the pond a couple of times thinking. Then he walked straight to the office of Jim Judge, the archaeologist in charge of a big National Park Service study of Chaco Canyon. Studies like the one Betancourt had in mind cost money, so he persuaded Judge to give him a research grant. Then Betancourt called Tom Van Devender, the University of Arizona scientist who was the leading expert on pack rat midden studies. One thing led to another, and soon Betancourt had transferred to the University of Arizona to study with Van Devender. In the summer of 1979, Betancourt led a group of people to Chaco Canyon to collect pack rat middens.

What they found was amazing. Most of the middens had piñon in them. Betancourt's observation that day on the cliff had been right—this was the sort of place that piñon-juniper woodland can grow. Why were those trees gone?

Betancourt and Tom Van Devender collecting pack rat middens at Chaco Canyon.

Betancourt's team sent the samples to the carbon-dating laboratory to see how old each midden was. He remembers the excitement when the test results came back. "We got the dates back and we realized that we had a very interesting story," he says.

For much of the last 11,000 years, the middens reflected the region's changing climate. Like Douglass's tree rings and Elrick's layers of sediment, the middens are a great paleoclimate record. As the climate got wetter or drier, the kinds of plants that grew around the pack rats' caves changed. Ten thousand years ago, as the planet was emerging from the last *ice age*, the climate around Chaco Canyon was cooler and wetter. Big Douglas firs and blue spruce grew there then.

By 6,000 years ago, the climate had dried out and warmed up, and the piñon-juniper woodland had taken over. Betancourt also found the first appearances of small plants that need summer rains to survive. That seemed to show a shift to a climate similar to today's. Summer rains—the

How Climate Changed the Trees on Dutch John Mountain

Dutch John Mountain, in northern Utah, is a special place for understanding climate in the western United States. It lies on a line separating the warm, dry desert lands to the south from the cooler, wetter forests to the north. The line is fuzzy, and where you draw it depends on how you define the differences between the desert and the forest. One definition is the extent of piñon pine, one of the classic trees of the desert Southwest.

One way of measuring how climate changes over thousands of years is to measure the spread of plants like piñon across the landscape. Trees can't move in the same way as animals or people, and they respond much more slowly to changing climate. They drop new seeds nearby or have them carried by birds, mammals, or the wind to a new spot. If the climate is favorable there, they can grow and spread. If not, they die. In that way, they respond to changes in climate.

As the climate warmed and dried in the centuries following the end of the last ice age, piñon pine slowly moved north. Dutch John Mountain is the farthest the piñons got. The story of how they got there shows how climate and *ecosystems*, changing over long periods, bring us the landscape we see today.

Julio Betancourt and Stephen Gray used pack rat middens to figure out when the piñon pines got to Dutch

North American *monsoon*—provide a big part of Chaco's annual precipitation.

But the big surprise came when Betancourt tracked the end of the piñon-juniper woodland. The pack rat middens showed the trees were there when the Anasazi, the native people who disappeared from Chaco Canyon, first arrived. But by the time the Anasazi left, the piñon-juniper woodland was also gone. Other studies didn't show any climate change big enough to explain the loss of the trees. But Betancourt remembered that November day years before when he had stood on the cliff looking down at Pueblo Bonito. "November in Chaco Canyon can be brutally cold," he says. "I thought, Where did they get the wood to keep warm?"

Studying ancient climates is interesting. But Betancourt's studies of the effects of climate and population at Chaco Canyon captured public attention in a different way than climate studies usually do. The studies weren't just about climate; they were about people. "We want to know a lot about our ancestors," he says.

Could the people who lived at Chaco Canyon have cut down all the trees? Drought had always seemed the most obvious explanation for the abandonment of Chaco Canyon. Could something else have happened?

"Although drought may have contributed, the Anasazi themselves also inflicted fatal blows on the fragile desert environment," famous scientist Jared Diamond wrote.

One of the best definitions of *drought* comes from Kelly Redmond, a scientist in Reno, Nevada, who has studied climate in the western United States his whole life. Kelly defines it as "insufficient water to meet needs." That means two things matter: how much rain and snow fall from the sky and how animals and plants—including humans—use it. If population grows, a city needs more water, whether that city is ancient Chaco Canyon or modern Las Vegas. A dry spell that might not pose problems for a small population can be devastating when the population grows too large.

At Chaco Canyon, the population 900 years ago had grown dramatically. Added to that, the people living there had cut down the trees. The weather got dry for a long time, but no longer than previous dry spells the ancient people had lived through. This time, though, the combination of problems—less water, fewer trees, more people—was enough to drive them from Chaco Canyon forever.

Betancourt recording data about one of the pack rat middens he collected in Chaco Canyon.

Perhaps the people who lived at Chaco Canyon cut down all the trees.

John Mountain. They used tree rings to figure out what the climate was like when it happened.

The evidence suggests the first piñon pine got to Dutch John Mountain in the mid-1200s. The piñons made a big jump to get there. The nearest site inhabited by piñon pine at the time was 25 miles (40 kilometers) away. But the trees had a hard time of it. After they arrived, a deep drought set in that lasted from 1250 to 1288. This famous drought is called "the Great Drought" by archaeologists and tree ring scientists. That's when the great Anasazi cities of Mesa Verde were abandoned.

On Dutch John Mountain, the Great Drought seems to have made life hard for the piñon pine. But Gray and Betancourt think the drought made life even harder for the Utah juniper, which had been the dominant tree on the mountain for nearly 10,000 years. When the weather got wet again, piñon pine quickly took over. Over the next few hundred years, the piñon pine took advantage of similar wet-dry cycles to become the dominant tree on Dutch John Mountain.

Measuring Snow

The depth of the snow following a big storm is one of the most talked-about weather measurements, but it's also one of the most misunderstood. People will often talk about how much snow fell in their yard. But unless they actually measure it, they're only guessing. And usually, as you will find out when you do this activity, they guess wrong, overestimating the amount of snow that fell.

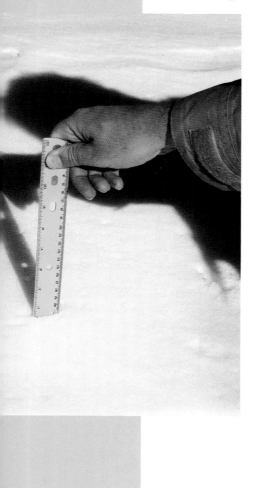

Measuring snow.

For this activity, the first thing you need is a snowstorm. If you live in a place that is too warm or too dry, you won't have a chance to try this.

You will need:

1. A snowstorm

2. A ruler

3. Your rain gauge

4. A large kitchen bowl

5. Your notebook

First, you will need to measure the depth of the snow. Take your ruler with you outside. Look for places where the snow has fallen on a flat surface, like a picnic table or the top of a car. It should be away from buildings. Stick the ruler straight down through the snow. Note the height of the top of the snow on the ruler.

Take three measurements, noting them in your journal.

For example,

- Measurement 1: 4 inches

- Measurement 2: 3 ½ inches

- Measurement 3: 4 ¼ inches

To determine the snow depth, you will need to take the average of the three measurements. To do this, add up the three numbers and divide by three.

- 4 + 3 ½ + 4 ½ = 12 inches

- $^{12}/_3$ = 4 inches

The average snow depth is four inches. Convert that to millimeters (multiply by 25.4). How many millimeters is it?

In addition to measuring the snow's depth, you also want to know how much water is in it. Four inches of light, fluffy snow has a lot less water than four inches of wet, slushy snow. That matters when you want to know how much water there is to melt and run off into streams and rivers.

This is the tricky part. Take the kitchen bowl outside with you to your rain gauge. The snow will have fallen into the opening. It may also have piled up on top of the rain gauge. Carefully pick the rain gauge up, being careful to get all the snow that has fallen on top of it. Dump the contents of the rain gauge and the snow on top of it into the kitchen bowl and take the bowl inside.

Let the snow melt, then pour it into the rain gauge. This will tell you how much actual water was in the snow that fell.

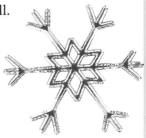

CHAPTER SIX

Henri Grissino-Mayer

Reading Stories in the Tree Rings

Henri Grissino-Mayer was looking for old trees. What he found, with a bit of luck and a lot of hard work, unlocked 2,000 years of climate history.

Grissino-Mayer was a scientist at the University of Arizona's Laboratory for Tree Ring Research. He was working on a survey of El Malpais, a *volcanic badland* near Grants, New Mexico. Trees can be great storytellers for a scientist like Grissino-Mayer, who knows how to read them. The older the tree is, the longer the story it can tell.

One of the staff at El Malpais was hiking through the rugged volcanic rocks looking for the remains of an old airplane wreck when he stumbled on exactly what Grissino-Mayer was looking for.

A scientist like Grissino-Mayer doesn't often find a tree as old as the one he named Yoda. Like its Star Wars namesake, the Yoda tree was very short, very gnarled, and very old. But amazingly, when Grissino-Mayer and his colleagues began collecting wood from Yoda and the other trees growing on the lava, they found many trees that were even older. Their lucky find opened a

Andy Bundshuh with the tree called Yoda, an ancient Douglas fir that yielded clues to New Mexico's ancient climate.

window on the climate history of New Mexico.

Grissino-Mayer remembers seeing his first tree rings when he was just two years old, on a visit to the local *arboretum* with his father. Each year, a tree puts on a new layer of growth. Cut right and carefully sanded off so you can see the rings, they are beautiful, like ripples flowing outward from the center of a pond.

A. E. Douglass, the founder of tree ring science, realized perfectly happy trees aren't much good. If you give a tree good soil and the ability to get water even in dry years, a growing season of the right length, and enough sunlight, it will prosper. Every year, it will put on a big, fat growth ring. It grows no matter how much rain and snow falls. That's no good for tree ring scientists like Douglass or Grissino-Mayer. They need trees that are in a little bit of trouble. Not enough trouble to kill them, but enough so that in a dry year, they put on a thin growth ring instead of a thick one. "We want the tortured ones" is how Grissino-Mayer puts it.

It's hard to imagine a tree with a tougher life than Yoda. Living on a *lava flow*, Yoda had no dirt to live in. It snaked its roots instead into pockets where rainwater collected in the rock. Few other plants were able to live on the lava at all, but Yoda and the other Douglas fir trees endured. A Douglas fir in the nearby mountains can grow a hundred feet (30 meters) tall. Yoda was just five feet (1.5 meters) tall and about one foot (0.3 meter) in diameter. But when Grissino-Mayer carefully extracted a core and counted Yoda's rings, he found that the tree was nearly 600 years old. Nearby, he found another Douglas fir, still alive, that was 1,275 years old. Another tree that had died in the 1860s had been an

Tree rings radiate outward like ripples on a pond.

Henri Grissino-Mayer screws a hollow tube into a tree to extract a tree-ring core.

Scientists use chain saws to get samples from fallen trees.

amazing 1,889 years old when it perished. Grissino-Mayer had found a mother lode of old trees.

To get tree ring data from a living tree, Grissino-Mayer screws a hollow metal core into the tree. He removes a long, thin piece of wood about as thick as a pencil. It doesn't hurt the tree—the tiny hole seals itself in a matter of weeks. The core is taken back to the lab and glued into what is called a *core mount*. The scientist then carefully sands it down. He looks just like a carpenter working on a beautiful piece of furniture. Carefully, he or she sands until the wood's grain is visible. Under a microscope, Grissino-Mayer measures the width of each tree ring. He needs a microscope because a tree like Yoda, 600 years old but tiny, grows very little every year. With a diameter of just a foot, the average tree ring on Yoda is just 1/100th of an inch. Some rings, the ones grown in the driest years, are far tinier.

Yoda's pattern of fat and thin rings is like an ancient calendar. To see the general pattern is easy. In 1871, the year the Colorado River was so low John Wesley Powell's boat trip was easy, Yoda and the other Malpais trees put on thin rings. The following year, their rings were much larger. That was the year the Colorado flooded so much that Powell and his team had to abandon the rest of their journey. El Malpais is hundreds of miles from the headwaters of the Colorado River, but climate effects are widespread. That's why rings from well-chosen trees are such a useful tool to scientists like Grissino-Mayer.

The next step is to use the measurements to turn the width of Yoda's rings into a rain gauge. This isn't as easy as it sounds.

It might seem obvious that a tree like Yoda would grow a fatter ring in a wet year and a narrower ring in a dry year. But how much rain does it take to create a ring of a certain width? Sometimes assuming the obvious turns out to be wrong. Scientists like Grissino-Mayer have to be careful that their assumptions are correct.

To find out the truth about the tree rings, Grissino-Mayer turned to a branch of mathematics known as *statistics*. Statistics involves clever mathematical formulas used to calculate how closely the patterns of fat and thin rings compare to rain gauge records for the area collected since 1895. Grissino-Mayer figured out that the ring widths most closely match the amount of *precipitation*—rain and snow—from one summer to the next. The more rain and snow that fell, the fatter the ring.

The ring widths and precipitation numbers didn't match up perfectly. But the statisticians' mathematical tool kit allowed Grissino-Mayer to calculate how close the match was. It also allowed him to come up with a formula to use tree ring widths to estimate how much precipitation had fallen each year before there were any rain gauges to measure it.

An accurate result takes more than one tree. One tree might have quirks. One year insects might attack it, stunting its growth and leaving a thin ring. That might trick a scientist into thinking there had been a drought. Or a flood might have washed dirt away from the tree's roots and the tree would have had trouble growing. That could trick a scientist into thinking there had been a drought when really the year had been wet. Statisticians call this the difference between "signal" and "noise." Think of sitting in a crowded restaurant and trying to listen to what the person sitting across the table from you is saying. His or her conversation is the signal. The sound of plates clanging and babies crying around the room is noise. Out at El Malpais, the climate is the conversation Grissino-Mayer is trying to listen to—the signal. All the rest—insects, fires, floods, and the like—is noise.

Scientists' solution to the noise problem is usually to collect more data. One tree may have been attacked by insects, but if you collect

Trees under stress, living in arid climates, make the best subjects for tree ring climate studies.

Stradivarius and Climate

The sound of violins made in Italy three centuries ago in Italy, like this one, are legendary. Grissino-Mayer studied the tree rings in the wood used to make them and concluded climate may have had something to do with the unique sound.

Tree rings are good for studying more than just climate. In one unusual example, Henri Grissino-Mayer has applied his science to the history of music.

Violins made in the 1600s and early 1700s are legendary. The most famous violin maker of all time was Italian Antonio Stradivari. Great concert violinists sometimes spend more money for their instrument than they do for their house. In 2006, a Stradivarius violin sold for $3.5 million. Musicians say Stradivarius violins sound better. Why?

Grissino-Mayer and a colleague, Lloyd Burckle, think tree rings hold the

enough tree ring measurements from enough separate places, most trees won't have been attacked by insects that year. That's why tree ring scientists want lots of trees to measure, 20 trees minimum. Thirty is better. In El Malpais, Grissino-Mayer and the team of scientists he worked with collected 240 samples. In addition to coring live trees, they took pieces of dead wood they found lying on the ground back to their Tucson laboratory.

Using all of the trees, Grissino-Mayer created a record of climate for northwestern New Mexico stretching back 2,129 years. That's before the rise of the Roman Empire in Europe. In what is now the southwestern United States, the great Anasazi culture hadn't yet been born.

Grissino-Mayer's record of northwestern New Mexico climate is a remarkable testament to the way climate changes. It shows the sort of year-to-year variations that caused John Wesley Powell so much trouble when he first explored the Colorado River. It also shows long-term changes—droughts and wet spells that lasted decades or even centuries.

For example, from AD 661 to 1023, the climate was dry. Then it got wet for more than 300 years. That 300-year wet spell marked the rise of the Anasazi culture. But Grissino-Mayer's record shows something other scientists have also seen in the tree ring record. Within those centuries-long wet spells can be incredibly dry years or even dry decades. It was in the midst of that long wet spell, for example, that a pair of decade-long droughts contributed to the collapse of Anasazi society.

Once he had figured out the climate history of El Malpais, Grissino-Mayer wanted to expand his tree ring record across New Mexico. Working with a team of colleagues, he collected tree samples from the top of the Sandia Mountains, which rise above Albuquerque. The team also went to the Magdalena Mountains, in south-central New Mexico near the town of Socorro. At each site, they looked for the same thing they had found in El Malpais. They wanted trees living at the limit, tortured trees that would show the signs of drought in the width of their rings.

The three sites combined gave Grissino-Mayer and his colleagues 605 trees to work with. The three sites were far enough apart that the scientists were able to estimate what climate had been like for nearly 1,400 years in the Middle Rio Grande Valley—the most populated region of New Mexico. Just like at El Malpais, the Middle Rio Grande Valley has been subject to tremendous climate *variability*.

For human societies, what matters most isn't the average rain and snowfall every year. If you live in a dry climate, you can adjust. Problems happen in the years that are far above average (scientists call them *pluvials*) and far below average—droughts. In the Middle Rio Grande, Grissino-Mayer found many of both. In the 1,400 years he studied, he found 60 periods lasting five years or longer when the climate was either extremely wet or extremely dry.

To understand what those stretches meant to the people who lived here, a good place to visit is Gran Quivira. The Indian ruin southeast of Albuquerque was inhabited by a people called the Tompiro, who

The wood grain from an old Italian violin.

answer. Stradivari's great violins were made during the period scientists call the Maunder minimum. Lasting from 1645 to 1715, it was a time when the sun was less active. It was cooler in Europe, where the violins were being made.

Burckle and Grissino-Mayer think long winters and cool summers affected the trees, causing them to grow more slowly and evenly. The wood in a violin amplifies and echoes the sound made by the strings. Better wood makes better sound.

An old El Malpais tree stump shows
ragged growth rings, telling the story
of its hardscrabble past.

lived there for more than a thousand years. When the Spanish arrived in about 1600, they found a thriving village at Gran Quivira. Seventy years later, all the residents of Gran Quivira were gone. This is where tree rings stop being a simple measurement of how much a tree grew and become part of a human drama.

The trees show that for much of the first half of the 1600s, the climate at Gran Quivira was wet and stable. The Spanish took advantage of that, building small communities alongside the Tompiro and the other Native American communities that made their homes in the region. The Spanish taxed the Indians, forcing them to pay in food and labor.

This worked during the good times, when the climate supported good crops of corn and other staples on which the Indians depended. Then in the 1650s, the weather changed. The tree rings started shrinking in a drought. The tree rings got fatter again for a few years before a wicked drought set in beginning in 1666. The climate didn't get wet again for eight years. In modern times, when we have a drought in the United States, we can get food from other parts of the country where conditions are better. But in a society that depends on the food grown nearby, a drought like the one in 1666 can be disaster. And it was. Hundreds of people at Gran Quivira died of starvation, and the rest left. The people who had made their home in the region for a thousand years were gone.

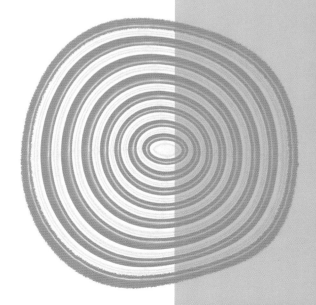

Albedo

Chances are good that you've already noticed what scientists call *albedo*. Have you ever walked barefoot outside on a sunny day and noticed how much warmer blacktop pavement is than the light-colored sidewalk? That's the result of albedo, which is one of the most important aspects underlying meteorology.

The albedo of an object is simply how much of the sun's energy the object reflects back into space and how much it absorbs, heating up in the process. In this activity, you can use a simple type of thermometer to measure the heat of various objects in the sun and learn how changing the albedo can have a dramatic effect on weather and climate.

Albedo is a measure of how much of the sun's energy an object reflects. Light-colored objects reflect more of the sun's energy, and so they have a high albedo. Dark-colored objects absorb more of the sun's energy, heating up, and so they have a low albedo.

Special thermometers can measure the *infrared radiation* emitted by an object. The hotter the object, the more infrared radiation it emits.

For this experiment, you will need an inexpensive *infrared thermometer*. This kind of thermometer is used in construction and is available at hardware stores or stores that sell electronics.

You will need:

1. An infrared thermometer

2. A sunny day

3. A snowy day

4. A snow shovel

5. Your journal

On a sunny day, take your thermometer outside and measure the temperature of black pavement. Now compare it to the temperature of a light-colored sidewalk nearby. Try various other surfaces. One of the most interesting comparisons is different-colored cars parked in the sun. How does the temperature of a dark-colored car differ from the temperature of a silver car or a white car? Why do you think the temperatures are so different?

One of the most important effects of albedo on weather happens when snow is covering the ground. Snow is white and reflects 75 to 95 percent of the sun's light. By comparison, a dry dirt field reflects anywhere from 5 to 20 percent of the sun's light. That means much more of the sun's energy is absorbed by the dry field, heating up the ground more.

In January 2007, a huge storm blanketed Albuquerque with a layer of snow that took days to melt. Nearby Gallup, New Mexico, didn't get snow. Gallup, which is higher in elevation, is usually colder than Albuquerque. But for days, Gallup was as much as 15 degrees *Fahrenheit* (eight degrees *Celsius*) warmer than Albuquerque. The reason: with no snow on it, the ground in Gallup absorbed sunlight and warmed up. The snow in Albuquerque reflected most of the sunlight back into space, keeping things much colder.

Infrared thermometer measuring the temperature of the pavement.

Here is another albedo experiment you can try if you live in a place with snow. When the sun comes out after a snowstorm, go out with your shovel and cut a hole in the snow so the sunlight can reach the pavement on a sidewalk or driveway. Watch how the snow warms up the pavement and begins melting the surrounding snow. Compare that area to one where there are no holes in the snow. The snow there will melt much more slowly.

CHAPTER SEVEN

El Niño

Every month during the winter, surveyors fan out across the mountains of the western United States to measure the snow. Sometimes they ride snowmobiles, ski or snowshoe, or fly into remote mountain sites by helicopter.

Workers push a tube into the snow in order to measure its depth.

To measure the snow, the surveyors take a long aluminum tube and push it down through the snow until it hits the ground. Markings on the tube tell them how deep the snow is. But knowing the depth of the snow doesn't tell them how much water it contains. A foot of light, fluffy snow holds less water than a foot of heavy, wet snow. The tube is open on the bottom so when the surveyors pull it up, it will be filled with snow. After measuring the snow's depth, they weigh the tube, which tells them how much water is in the snow.

James Church made the first snow survey in 1910, measuring the snow on Mount Rose, near Lake Tahoe, in Nevada. He wanted the data to forecast the flow of water into the lake.

More than a thousand sites are now regularly measured for the snow survey of the western states. Sitting in an office overlooking the Willamette River in Portland, Oregon, Tom Pagano waits patiently for the results. Pagano is a US government stream flow forecaster. His job is to analyze the information collected by the snow surveyors and forecast how much water will flow down streams and rivers in the western United States. At least once a month, beginning each year in January and running through the summer, Pagano issues an eagerly awaited report. Water managers want to know how much water to expect so they can decide when to release water from dams. River rafters want to know what kind of whitewater-rafting conditions they can expect. Farmers need to know how much water they can expect to irrigate their crops. All of those things depend on how much snow is in the mountains during the winter and spring, waiting for the weather to warm so that it can melt and flow into the rivers of the West.

From his vantage point, Pagano and the others members of the stream flow forecast team have a unique perspective on weather, climate, and water in the western United States. They can use their snowpack data to look beyond individual storms and see climate across the entire West over the course of an entire season. And what they see is an interesting pattern.

Snow data have been collected for a long enough time that the forecasters can compare this year to past years. Is it wetter? Is it drier? They like to think in what they call *anomalies*—how different are the snow data this year compared to the data in an average year? That is what water users need to know. Can they expect more water than an average year or less?

Withdrawing the tube from the snow, workers prepare to weigh it.

After watching for enough years, scientists who study climate across the West have begun to see patterns. Often, when it was wet in the Cascade Mountains of the Pacific Northwest, it would be drier across the Southwest. When it was dry in the Cascades, the Southwest tended to be wet. What, they wondered, could cause such large-scale patterns?

All scientists build on the work of people who came before them. The scientific path that led to an understanding of the snowpack patterns in the West began in the 1800s. Terrible droughts and famines struck India, and millions of people died. The monsoon rains on which India's farmers depended to water their crops simply shut down.

Scientists, desperate to understand why, had a new tool. India was part of a British empire that spanned the globe, and as the British traveled, they set up weather stations. That gave scientists the first global weather data, although it was a shadow of what we have today.

All over the West, workers must measure the depth of snow and weigh it to see how much water it contains. The measurements are crucial for estimating how much water will flow down streams and rivers in the coming spring.

There were far fewer weather stations than we have now, and there were no satellites or the Internet to deliver data instantly. Scientists who wanted to study global weather had to wait months for records to arrive by mail from distant weather stations. But these weather stations nevertheless gave scientists their first chance to study weather around the world on any given day.

At first, the British weather stations didn't help them understand why the weather had changed so much and why so many people had died. The British scientists could measure droughts better than anyone in history, but they couldn't see a pattern. Finally, in the early 1900s, Sir Gilbert Walker, a British scientist in charge of weather observations in India, collected all the data and launched a massive number-crunching campaign. Today, the sort of work Walker did would be done on a computer. But in those days, a "computer" was a person doing calculations by hand. Walker hired an army of clerks in India to do his calculations. They compared weather measurements from around the world looking for a pattern.

It took Walker and his "computers" 20 years, but they finally found what they were looking for in data from barometers used to measure air pressure on both sides of the Pacific. The barometer is the same instrument John Wesley Powell used to measure the change in elevation as he traveled down the Colorado River. This time, scientists were using it for a different purpose—to understand global weather patterns.

High pressure and low pressure are key parts of how wind and weather move around the globe. Today, they are a common feature of the weather maps you see in the newspaper or on the nightly television news. In the late 1800s and early 1900s, little was known about them. But Walker's analysis seemed to show that they had something to do with the disastrous droughts in India. For months and months, air pressure in Australia would be high. At the same time, far across the ocean, air pressure in South America would be low. Today, we know that high pressure is associated with a great mound of dry air piled up over Asia, preventing the rains. In Walker's day, no one knew why the high pressure happened

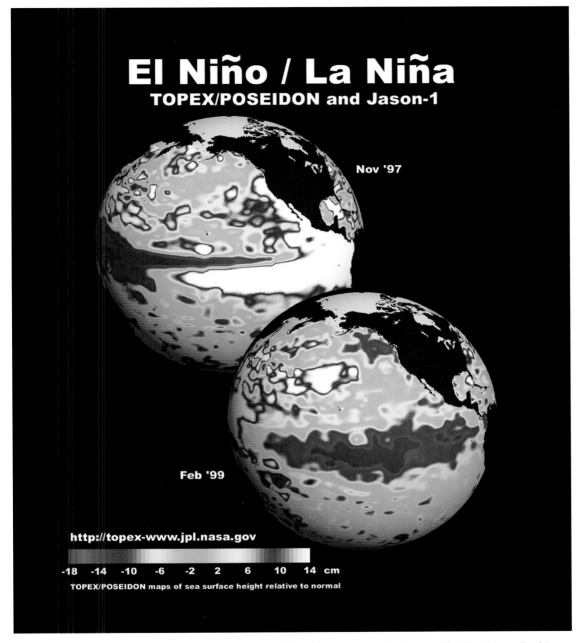

Satellites help scientists watch the vast Pacific Ocean, looking for patterns of cold and warm water that can help the scientists forecast whether the coming winter will be wet or dry.

or what it meant. But Walker realized that when it happened, India's monsoon would die.

Then, like a seesaw, the pattern would shift. Low air pressure in Australia was matched by high pressure across the ocean, in South America. The monsoon would resume. Seeing the seesaw in his data, Walker called it the "Southern Oscillation."

At the same time the monsoon rains failed, Walker's "computers" found changes in air pressure in Australia and all the way across the Pacific in South America. Climate all across the planet's largest ocean basin seemed to be linked. But how?

It took more than four decades for scientists to grasp the answer. That's when Norwegian meteorologist Jacob Bjerknes discovered a connection between changing ocean temperatures and the pressure changes Walker had found. Fishermen in Peru had long noticed changes in ocean temperatures during some winters. The changes came near Christmas, and the fishermen named them *El Niño*—"the little boy" in Spanish—after the birth of Christ, which they celebrated at that time of year. El Niño happens when the part of the Pacific Ocean along the equator gets unusually warm. Like a boulder diverting water in a stream, El Niño shifts currents that carry storms around the world, Bjerknes realized.

Scientists named the opposite pattern, when the water along the equator cooled, *La Niña*—"the little girl."

In North America, La Niña—the drought maker in the arid Southwest—pushes the storm track to the north. The Southwest, especially California, Arizona, and New Mexico, can still get storms in a La Niña year. But they tend to be fewer. As a result, the mountain snows the region depends on for its water are thinner. Plants and even cities can dry up.

One of the problems in studying El Niño and La Niña is similar to studying the history of drought. Records of ocean temperature and air pressure across the Pacific don't go back before the mid-1800s. But like

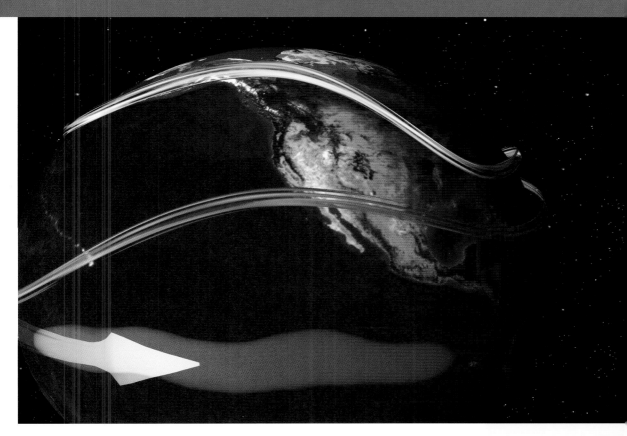

the tree ring scientists, researchers have found other ways of studying the history of the phenomenon.

One of the most important is coral, which grows in shallow ocean water. The tiny organisms grow in colonies that leave skeletons behind, creating great reefs in the process. As they grow, corals take up chemicals from their environment. As that environment changes, because of changing climate or for other reasons, differences show up in the coral skeleton. University of Arizona climate researcher Julie Cole's idea was to find a change made by El Niño and La Niña that would show up in the corals.

One of the things El Niño and La Niña do is shift rainfall patterns in the Pacific itself. Tarawa, an island 2,200 miles (3,500 kilometers) off the coast of Australia, is one of the places that get a lot wetter during an El Niño and drier during a La Niña. El Niño shifts storms in Tarawa's

When a pool of water warms across the Pacific Ocean (bottom, orange band), the jet stream (middle, pink band) is pulled over the southwestern United States, bringing winter storms with it. Called El Niño, it tends to cause wet winters across the Southwest as a result.

direction that normally rain on the Indian Ocean to the west. All that freshwater from rain changes the seawater, and Cole found a way to detect the differences in the skeletons left behind by the growing coral.

Cole and her colleagues found that they could use the corals to track the ebb and flow of El Niño and La Niña. The record left in the coral skeletons matches what the tree rings say about great droughts and wet spells across North America.

El Niño and La Niña aren't a perfect forecasting tool. If they were, surveyors would have no need to measure snow in the mountains—Pagano could just use the conditions in the Pacific Ocean to forecast the spring runoff. Even with El Niño and La Niña, conditions vary from year to year. But in recent years, scientists who study the snowpack have begun to notice something else about the climate that wasn't there before.

Phil Mote, who studies climate at the University of Washington in Seattle, looked at the average amount of snow on April 1 around the western United States. April 1 is usually the date when the snowpack reaches its peak—if you have to pick one day of the year to use to estimate how much river runoff there will be, April 1 is it. Mote compared the data collected by the snow surveyors every year since 1916. He found that El Niño and La Niña explain a big part of the year-to-year differences in how much snow fell in the mountains, providing the West with its water supplies. But in the last 50 years, April 1 snowpack has been declining.

As Mote looked for an explanation, he found one consistent pattern that could account for the declining snowpack. Snow needs cold weather. As the temperature rises, more precipitation falls as rain rather than snow. The snow line—the point where snow stops as you come down a mountain—moves higher. And over the past 50 years, temperatures around the world have been rising. Mote thinks global warming is the reason the snowpack in the West is declining.

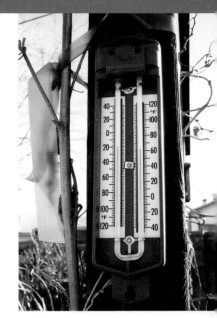

CHAPTER SEVEN **ACTIVITY**

Graphing Your Data

Once you have collected data, making a graph is one of the best ways to understand what the data are telling you. Scientists frequently use graphs to visualize their data.

You will need:

1. Your journal, with daily temperature data you have collected over a month or more

2. Graph paper

3. Colored pencils

U-shaped thermometer.

On the graph paper, mark the temperature range along the left-hand side. You need space to accommodate the lowest temperature you saw for the month, all the way up to the highest temperature. Scientists call this vertical scale the *y*-axis.

Along the bottom, mark the days of the month. Scientists call this horizontal scale the *x*-axis.

For each day, make a mark showing the high and low temperature. It will be easiest to read the graph if you use different-colored pencils for the low and the high. Don't worry if you missed a day checking the temperatures. Sometimes you'll be too busy or get sick. Just plot the data you have.

Once you have plotted each day's low temperature, use your colored pencils to draw a line connecting those temperatures. Then go back and do the same thing for each day's high temperature. Do your data show any patterns? Were there any warm spells, where the line goes up high on your graph? Were there any cold spells, where the line went down low?

Graph of high and low temperatures.

CHAPTER EIGHT

Connie Woodhouse

Using Trees to Help Think about the Future

Connie Woodhouse.

The problems of climate in the western United States come together at a place called Lee's Ferry. There, amid the red rock deserts of northern Arizona, is the most important measuring gauge on the Colorado River. Few people understand the problems to be found there in quite the same way as Connie Woodhouse. Her tool kit will be familiar by now—Woodhouse studies tree rings.

The Colorado, which made John Wesley Powell famous, is the most important river in the *arid* West. Most of the Colorado's water comes from small creeks high in the Rocky Mountains. The creeks collect the melting snow and funnel it south into the great deserts of the West.

The Colorado's *watershed* spreads over 246,000 square miles (632,000 square kilometers). If you compare the Colorado to its bigger cousins to the east, the river itself seems small. The Mississippi River is more than 40 times bigger than the Colorado. That's because much of the Colorado's watershed is dry. For the people who live in the watershed, that makes the Colorado even more important. Much of the country along the Mississippi River's route is wet enough to grow crops with the rain that falls from the sky. Almost none of the land in the Colorado River basin is wet enough to do that.

Glen Canyon Dam today holds back the Colorado River's water upstream from Lee's Ferry, where the river's water is measured.

Huge dams collect and store the Colorado River's water. A spiderweb of canals delivers it to seven western states. Cities like Las Vegas and Los Angeles couldn't exist without it. The vast farms of central Arizona and California's Imperial Valley would be impossible. Albuquerque also gets water from the Colorado River Basin. It comes through a pipe that carries it beneath the mountains, dumping it into the Rio Grande. Water in the West often travels a long way from the river where it starts to the places where people use it. But because the West is a dry place, the Colorado doesn't have water to spare. So a spiderweb of laws even more complex than the canals determines who gets how much. At Lee's Ferry, scientists measure the river's flow to see who gets how much.

Water blasts from the base of Glen Canyon Dam.

Lee's Ferry is at the end of a narrow, winding road. Today, it has a quiet campground and a boat ramp. Rafters gather to start trips through the Grand Canyon. In John Wesley Powell's day, the river at Lee's Ferry could be a raging torrent during the heavy spring snow-melt. In autumn, the Colorado often dropped to a gentle flow. Today, humans control the Colorado. At Lee's Ferry, it's a winding ribbon of tame green water. Glen Canyon Dam, 15 miles (24 kilometers) upstream, releases water past Lee's Ferry in a slow, steady flow. When I rafted down the river with a group of scientists, the only change in the Colorado's flow came every afternoon. Glen Canyon Dam's managers would increase the flow to generate electricity for air conditioners in cities around the West.

Almost all of the Colorado River's water starts as snow. It falls in the mountains of Wyoming, Colorado, Utah, and New Mexico. All of the things we have been talking about in this book—climate, snow-fall and snowmelt, and the needs of living creatures—come together there. The temperature of the Pacific Ocean and its interaction with the atmosphere pushes and pulls the *jet stream*, which brings storms across North America. The jet stream determines how much snow falls in the mountains. The snowfall, in turn, determines how much water ends up in the Colorado. In 1869, the snowfall determined how much water carried John Wesley Powell down the river. Today, it determines how much there is to fill the dams and canals, to water the crops, and to fill the drinking fountains of a thirsty West.

The government leaders who gathered in 1922 to divvy up the Colorado River's water picked Lee's Ferry as the dividing line. Their plan, called the Colorado River Compact, said that upstream states— Wyoming, Colorado, Utah, and New Mexico—would get half of the river's water. Downstream states—Nevada, Arizona, and California— would get the other half. The question was how much water everyone could expect.

One of our recurring themes has been the lack of long-term data about weather and climate. That was the problem in 1922. A. E. Douglass's tree ring research was just beginning. So the commission developing the Colorado River Compact had just 20 years of stream gauge data to determine the Colorado River's average flow. They had no scientific tools to help them estimate what had come before. Their best guess, based on the limited data at hand, was that the Colorado carried an average of about 17.5 million *acre-feet* (21.6 million cubic meters) per year of water. Acre-feet is the standard measure for large quantities of water in the United States—enough to cover an acre of land with water one foot deep. (An acre-foot is equal to 326,000 gallons, or 1.2 million liters.) One way of thinking of the Colorado River's water is that 17.5 million acre-feet of water is enough to cover the entire state of New Mexico in water nearly three inches (nearly seven centimeters) deep. The commissioners estimated that if the upstream states used 7.5 million acre-feet per year and passed along 7.5 million acre-feet of water past Lee's Ferry to the downstream states, there would be enough water to meet the needs of the growing West. At the time, they ignored Mexico's needs.

The Colorado River commissioners understood that the river would have more water in some years and less in others. They established a formula that allowed the upstream states to make up for dry years by delivering more water in wet years. But they didn't account for the possibility that the Colorado River had less or more water to begin with than they'd thought. What if the region was drier or wetter than they realized? If it was wetter, it wouldn't be a problem. But what if the 20 years they used as the basis for the allocation was drier than average? What if over time, there really wasn't that much water in the river to begin with?

Woodhouse is a member of the latest generation of tree ring scientists who have tried to answer the question: How much water did the Colorado River carry in the past?

Woodhouse came to the stream flow business by accident. Working at a *paleoclimate* data center in Boulder, Colorado, she did a small study of the flow on Boulder Creek. The creek flows out of the Rocky Mountains into the center of town and provides part of the city's water supply.

Woodhouse's tree ring stream flow studies are very similar to the estimates of past rainfall pioneered by A. E. Douglass. She goes out into the field to sample tree sites in the mountains where a river's snowpack falls.

Woodhouse used tree ring measurements from the mountains around Boulder Creek and compared the ring widths to measured flow in Boulder Creek back to 1912, when the first stream gauge was installed in the creek. That allowed her to develop a mathematical formula relating tree ring width to flow in Boulder Creek.

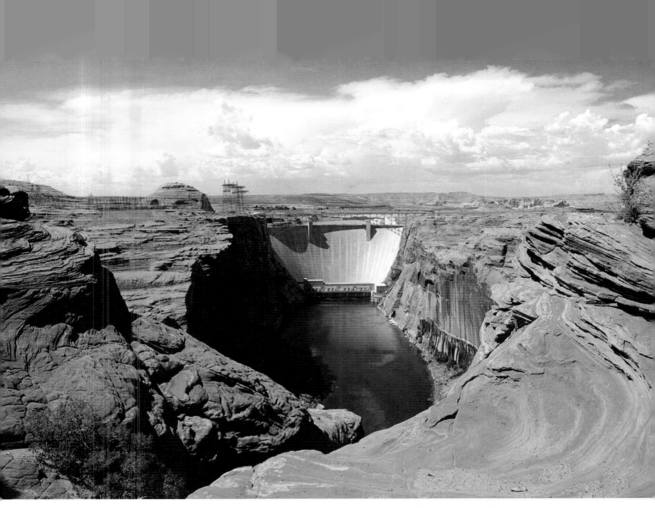

Glen Canyon Dam.

Applying the formula to older tree rings, she was able to estimate the flow in Boulder Creek all the way back to 1703.

The results were startling. The city of Boulder's ideas about the worst droughts it could expect to see were based on the record since 1912. Woodhouse found that there had been times in the not-too-distant past when drought had been far worse. From 1844 to 1852, the creek had been far drier.

The project didn't get much attention at first. Then in 2002, a drought set in across the West. Suddenly, water managers took notice of the tree ring studies. The city of Denver's water department asked Woodhouse and her colleagues to do a study for them on the flows of

Ed Schulman (left) takes a core sample from a tree as A. E. Douglass, the founder of tree ring science, looks on. Schulman made the first attempt to use tree rings to calculate past flows on the Colorado River.

the rivers that supply rapidly growing Denver. For years, Woodhouse had been making summer trips through the Rocky Mountains, collecting tree rings samples a week at a time. It was like a fun camping vacation in the woods for her. When Denver officials called with questions, Woodhouse already had the data to answer them. "A lot of this is really being at the right place at the right time," Woodhouse said. The results for Denver were similar to those for Boulder. The rivers that supply Denver's water had been in droughts far worse than anything the city's water managers realized.

The first attempt to estimate the Colorado River's long-term flow was done by Edmund Schulman in the 1940s. The river's managers needed more information about the river's long-term flow to tell how reliable the electricity supply from Hoover Dam would be. The dam's power was critical to factories building airplanes during World War II. Schulman's techniques were crude by today's standards—he used fewer trees, and he didn't have computers to analyze all the numbers. His results suggested that the river had been unusually wet when the Colorado Compact estimates were made. But his work had little impact.

The first estimate of the Colorado River's long-term flow that attracted serious attention was done in 1976 by Charles Stockton and Gordon Jacoby. Jacoby worked at the University of Arizona's Laboratory of Tree Ring Research—the institution started by tree ring pioneer A. E. Douglass and the same place Schulman had done his work. Stockton and Jacoby's research also showed how unusually wet the Colorado had been in the 20 years used to determine the Colorado River Compact divisions. Their estimate showed that the Colorado was subject to droughts far worse than anything seen in the 20th century. Among scientists, their work is famous. But water resource managers at the turn of the 21st century paid little attention to what Stockton and Jacoby had found.

When another massive drought set in during 2005, people started listening. Woodhouse was again in the right place at the right time. She had already collected tree ring samples across Colorado, and a colleague had samples from the high country of Utah, which also feeds the Colorado River. Woodhouse assembled a team and set out to update Stockton and Jacoby's famous reconstruction of the flow of the Colorado.

Their results show the Colorado River's problem. The framers of the Colorado River Compact picked the worst time to divide the river's water. The tree ring estimates show that the 20 years they based the Colorado River Compact on was the wettest period in the last 500 years.

But the most important message for Westerners may be the zigzags in Woodhouse's river flow graphs. In the 1600s, the 1700s, and again in the 1800s, the Colorado flowing past Lee's Ferry was drier than at any time in the

Equipment needed for the experiment.

SODA STRAWS

Not all science takes fancy, high-tech equipment. Connie Woodhouse and the other scientists at the Laboratory of Tree Ring Research in Tucson, Arizona, also depended for years on a local restaurant supply store called Uncle Bob's Popcorn. Woodhouse and her team also treasure empty Pringles potato chip cans.

Working out in the field, Woodhouse explains, you need a "system." Tree ring scientists need places to keep their tools and easy ways to carry them, pull them out, and use them when they need to. For old dead trees, tree ring scientists use a chain saw, which they use to cut out big wedges of wood. But the most important tool used by tree ring scientists is an increment borer—a hand drill used to extract pencil-thin cylinders of wood from the heart of a tree.

When they pull the core out, they need something to put it in. For years, that thing was the paper straws sold by Uncle Bob's. They were just the right size to hold the tiny core, and they had a wax coating that made it easy to slip in the wood. And they were just the right length to fit into a Pringles can.

Uncle Bob's paper straws are no longer made. Instead, Woodhouse and her colleagues use paper straws sold by art supply stores for craft projects. But when she was moving recently, Woodhouse found a stash of Uncle Bob's straws in her garage.

Woodhouse with one of the trees she uses to study the history of the West's climate.

20th century. The great industrial farms and cities have grown to depend on water that in the past just wasn't there. We apparently have been extraordinarily lucky.

Today, the people who manage the Colorado River are taking the tree ring estimates more seriously. A new plan for managing the Colorado River, published in 2007, includes the tree ring–based estimates of river flow developed by Woodhouse and her colleagues. The river's managers are using them to help figure out how to manage the water if we get another drought like the ones found in the tree ring record.

Preparing for drought is important in the West. While the tree ring record tells us there have been serious droughts in the past, the scientists who study *global warming* say droughts could get even worse in the future. Global warming is caused by pollution from factory smokestacks and the tailpipes of cars. Computer simulations show that the western United States is likely to get warmer over the next century. That means whatever rain and snow fall from the sky will evaporate more quickly, leaving even less water in the Colorado and the other rivers of the West.

If You Want to Know More about Western Climate . . .

WEBSITES

Western Regional Climate Center, www.wrcc.dri.edu
Run by the Desert Research Institute in Reno, the Western Regional Climate Center has the West's best collection of climate data. You can use it to find out what the normal rainfall in your community is each year, whether the temperatures have been rising, and whether this year is drier or wetter than normal.

Climate Assessment of the Southwest, www.climas.arizona.edu
Run by the University of Arizona, the Climate Assessment of the Southwest (CLIMAS) project provides up-to-date information on current weather, water supply, and forecasts for the coming season. CLIMAS specializes in taking complex climate data and translating it into forms that you don't need to be a scientist to understand.

El Niño Page, www.elnino.noaa.gov
The National Oceanic and Atmospheric Administration's El Niño page will tell you all about the phenomenon that has a lot to do with whether our climate is wet or dry. It also serves as a great jumping-off point for all things El Niño all over the Internet.

Weather, www.weather.gov
The National Weather Service, the federal government agency that brings you your forecasts every day, offers a starting point for all the weather data they collect from around the country. Find forecasts, the latest storms, and data from every one of the weather stations in the country they manage.

The Desert Laboratory, www.tumamoc.org
The oldest center for research into western desert climate and ecosystems, in Tucson.

BOOKS
(order through any bookstore)

Tree Rings and Telescopes: The Scientific Career of A. E. Douglass,
        by George Ernest Webb
This biography of A. E. Douglass, founder of tree ring science, shows the fits and starts and grand adventures that led Douglass to one of the most important scientific discoveries of the 20th century for western climate science.

The Exploration of the Colorado River and Its Canyons,
        by John Wesley Powell
Powell's diaries of his exploration of the Grand Canyon are part scientific journal and part grand adventure story.

Beyond the Hundredth Meridian, by Wallace Stegner
One of the West's great storytellers brings us the life of John Wesley Powell.

People of Chaco, by Kendrick Frazier
The story of Chaco Canyon, the people who lived there, and the archaeologists who have helped us understand them.

Glossary

acre-foot: The amount of water needed to cover an acre of land one foot deep. One acre-foot equals 326,000 gallons (1.2 million liters). Acre-feet is a common measure of water in the United States.

albedo: The amount of sunlight reflected by an object. A black object reflects little sunlight and heats up as a result of absorbing the sun's light. A white object warms less because it reflects more of the sun's light. Snow has a high albedo, reflecting so much sunlight that you might need sunglasses. A dark street, in comparison, absorbs the sunlight rather than reflecting it, warming the pavement.

anomaly: A change from normal or average. Climate scientists use anomalies to explain how unusually wet or dry, warm or cold the weather or climate is.

arboretum: A park where plants are studied and preserved, usually open for the public to see them.

archaeologist: A scientist who studies ancient humans. Archaeologists frequently try to understand climate during the time the people they study were alive.

arid: Dry. Regions with arid climates, like deserts, have less plant and animal life than regions with wet climates.

astronomer: A scientist who studies planets, stars, and galaxies beyond the earth. Some astronomers have studied the effect of the sun on the earth's climate.

atmosphere: The layer of air surrounding the earth.

barometer: An instrument to measure air pressure. Changes in air pressure signal changes in weather. Lower pressure usually means a storm is coming, and higher pressure usually means warmer, drier weather. Barometers also can be used to measure altitude. Air pressure is created by the weight of air above. It decreases as you go higher up a mountain, which is why it feels harder to breathe when you're high on a mountain.

cambium: The layer of growing tissue in a tree. Each year, the tree puts on a layer of cambium, which shows up as a ring.

carbon dating: A technique to determine how old something is. Some kinds of carbon change over time. Scientists know how fast it changes, so they can use it as a "molecular clock." A type of carbon known as *carbon-14* gradually changes over time into nitrogen. Measuring the amount of carbon-14 left in a sample of plant or animal tissue allows scientists to determine how long it has been since the organism died. Carbon dating can be used to date plants and animals up to about 50,000 years old.

Celsius: A metric scale of temperature measurement in common use around the world. Water freezes at 0 degrees Celsius, and 100 degrees Celsius is the boiling point of water at sea level. See *Fahrenheit*.

climate: The long-term average of daily weather conditions. Deserts have dry climates because it doesn't rain or snow very often. Jungles have wet climates because it rains a lot. Having a single rainy day in the desert or a single dry day in the jungle doesn't change the climate.

climate change: A change in the long-term average of weather patterns. The phrase *climate change* is most often used to describe the effect of greenhouse gases emitted by humans, which is also often called *global warming*. In the past, climate changed for natural reasons but much more slowly than today. See *pluvial.*

core mount: A holder used to mount a core sample taken from a tree in order to study tree rings.

drought: A period with less-than-average rain or snow. In an extremely wet climate, a few dry months can be called a drought. In a desert, it can take a year or more of unusually dry weather to qualify as a drought. Droughts also depend on how much water the plants, animals, and humans living in a place are accustomed to. One famous definition of drought is "insufficient water to meet needs." As the need for water changes—because a population grows, for example—the definition of drought can change along with it.

ecosystem: An interrelated group of plants, animals, and other living things that live together, each depending on the others.

El Niño: An unusual warming of the Pacific Ocean along the equator. It happens every two to seven years on average and brings changes in weather patterns around the world. See *La Niña.*

equator: The imaginary line around the earth's middle, separating the Northern and Southern hemispheres. The equator is generally the warmest place on earth because it receives the most sunlight.

evaporation: The process by which a liquid, especially water, turns into a gas.

Fahrenheit: A temperature scale used in the United States. Thirty-two degrees Fahrenheit is the freezing point of water, and 212 degrees is water's boiling point. Water boils more easily at higher elevations, so the boiling point is lower.

forecast model: A computer simulation of the earth's atmosphere used to help forecast the weather.

glacier: A permanent cap of snow and ice, usually on top of a mountain. Glaciers form when it's cold enough so snow that falls in the winter doesn't melt in the summer. Long-term changes in the climate change glaciers. As the planet warms because of *greenhouse gases*, glaciers are melting, making them smaller.

global warming: An increase in the earth's temperature caused by rising greenhouse gases.

graduate student: A student who has finished four years of college and is getting an advanced degree, usually a master's or a doctorate. Graduate students spend less time in class and more time doing original research.

greenhouse gases: Gases such as carbon dioxide (abbreviated CO_2) that hold heat near the earth's surface. Without naturally occurring greenhouse gases, the earth would be much colder. Greenhouse gases emitted when we burn gasoline and other fuels are making the earth warmer and changing its climate patterns.

heat engine: A system that is driven by heat moving from one place to another. A steam engine is a heat engine, moving heat from the boiler to the engine's wheels. The earth's climate is also a heat engine, driven by sunlight warming air and setting off a cascade of events that moves the air around the planet.

hemisphere: Half of the planet. The Northern Hemisphere includes Europe, Asia, and North America, where the majority of the earth's population lives. Africa, South America, Australia, and Antarctica are the major landmasses in the Southern Hemisphere.

high pressure: A large-scale weather pattern in which clear, dry air dominates. This weather pattern is called *high* pressure because the air pressure actually increases and dry descending air tends to keep clouds away. See *low pressure*.

ice age: A period in which the earth's climate is colder and ice covers large parts of the landmasses of the Northern Hemisphere. The most recent ice age ended about 11,600 years ago. Scientists think ice ages are caused by slight changes in the earth's orbit, which change how much sunlight falls during summer and winter.

infrared radiation: Like light but invisible to the human eye, infrared radiation is emitted by objects because of their heat. The earth's surface, after warming during the day, cools off at night by emitting infrared radiation.

infrared thermometer: A thermometer that measures the surface of an object by measuring the infrared radiation it emits.

jet stream: The river of high-altitude air that steers storms across the Northern and Southern hemispheres.

La Niña: An unusual cooling of the Pacific Ocean along the equator. It can lead to drought across the southern United States. See *El Niño*.

lava flow: When hot molten rock, called *lava*, rises through a volcano, it sometimes flows out across the landscape, leaving a rocky lava flow as it cools. The rocks are usually dark and often jagged and hard to walk across.

low pressure: A large-scale weather pattern in which air tends to flow in from surrounding areas, providing the lift to create storms.

Maunder minimum: A period from the mid-1600s to the early 1700s when sunspot activity declined. Changes in the sun's behavior have been linked to changes in the earth's climate.

maximum-minimum thermometer: A thermometer that keeps track of the high and low temperatures.

meteorologist: A scientist who studies the weather. People who do daily weather forecasts are usually meteorologists.

midden: A midden is nothing more than a trash pile, but it can be a scientific gold mine. Archaeologists study middens left by humans to figure out how they lived. Consider how much information a future scientist could get about you by digging through your trash 100 years from now. Climate scientists study pack rat middens to learn about the plants that grew around the pack rat's nest. Changing climate means different plants will be found in middens from different times.

molecule: One of the basic building blocks of all matter around us, a molecule is the smallest indivisible bit of matter in an object. It is made up of even smaller objects called atoms that are tightly bound together. In our atmosphere, for example, carbon dioxide, oxygen, and water are among the most important molecules to be found.

monsoon: A pattern of rain, usually in the summer, that happens when vast winds bring moist air off the ocean onto land. The Asian monsoon is the most famous: moist air sweeps across India toward the Himalayas. Northern Mexico and the southwestern United States also experience a summer monsoon in July and August that brings the region a large percentage of its precipitation.

paleoclimate: The study of climate in the time before thermometers and rain gauges. The scientists who specialize in the field are called paleoclimatologists. Among the techniques they use is the measurement of tree rings and rock layers to learn about the climate during the time they were formed.

pluvial: A long period with above-average rain and snow. The opposite of *drought*.

precipitation: Rain or snow.

radiosonde: An instrument carried aloft by a weather balloon that measures temperature, water vapor, and winds.

rain gauge: An instrument for measuring rainfall.

sea level: The level of the ocean. Sea level is closely tied to climate conditions. As the earth warms, less water is trapped in glaciers and other ice. The water flows to the ocean, and sea level rises. As the earth cools, the opposite happens: the sea level falls.

sedimentary rocks: Rocks formed when sediments fall to the bottom of a body of water. Layers of sedimentary rocks often leave clues about the climate of the time in which they were formed.

sounding: A measurement made by a weather balloon, which records temperature and humidity as it rises through the atmosphere. Ocean scientists also take soundings by lowering instruments into the water behind a boat, measuring temperature at various depths.

statistics: A branch of mathematics that deals with the collection and analysis of data. Statisticians have special mathematical techniques for looking for patterns in data, like whether daily temperatures are warming or whether long-term precipitation trends are going up or down.

sunspots: Dark spots on the surface of the sun that increase and decrease on an 11-year cycle. They cause slight changes in the amount of sunlight reaching the earth, resulting in a slight change in the earth's climate.

troposphere: The layer of the earth's atmosphere from sea level to about six miles (10 kilometers) above the earth's surface. The troposphere is where most of what we call weather happens.

ultralight: A tiny aircraft, small enough to carry one person in an open cockpit and used by scientists to take atmospheric measurements.

variability: Change above and below average. A region with high climate variability exhibits large differences between its wettest and driest years.

volcanic badland: A vast *lava flow* that is hard to walk on and even harder to live on.

watershed: The area in which rain and snow fall that eventually flow into a particular river.

weather: Daily atmospheric conditions. Wind, temperature, humidity, sunlight, cloud cover, rain, and snow are all part of weather. See *climate*.

Illustration Credits

Front cover:	Henri Grissino-Mayer (tree ring).
	Lissa Heineman (rain gauge).
	National Park Service (tree).
	John Fleck (pack rat).
page viii:	US Geological Survey.
page xii:	US Geological Survey.
page 2:	US Geological Survey.
page 2:	US Geological Survey.
page 2:	US Geological Survey.
page 3:	Library of Congress.
page 6:	NASA.
page 8:	US Geological Survey.
page 9:	National Park Service.
page 11:	John Fleck.
page 12:	Lissa Heineman.
page 13:	National Oceanic and Atmospheric Administration.
page 13:	National Oceanic and Atmospheric Administration.
page 14:	Lissa Heineman.
page 14:	Lissa Heineman.
page 14:	Lissa Heineman.
page 15:	National Oceanic and Atmospheric Administration.
page 16:	National Oceanic and Atmospheric Administration.
page 17:	Mel Strong.
page 19:	NASA.
page 20:	Lissa Heineman.
page 22:	Maya Elrick.

page 24:   John Fleck.

page 26:   Lissa Heineman.

page 26:   Lissa Heineman.

page 27:   Lissa Heineman.

page 27:   Lissa Heineman.

page 28:   Lissa Heineman.

page 29:   Lissa Heineman.

page 30:   David C. Mason.

page 31:   Laboratory of Tree Ring Research.

page 33:   Henri Grissino-Mayer.

page 34:   Laboratory of Tree Ring Research.

page 34:   National Park Service.

page 35:   Laboratory of Tree Ring Research.

page 36:   Lissa Heineman.

page 39:   David C. Mason.

page 40:   National Park Service.

page 41:   Julio Betancourt.

page 43:   Julio Betancourt.

page 43:   David C. Mason.

page 44:   Lissa Heineman.

page 46:   Henri Grissino-Mayer.

page 47:   Henri Grissino-Mayer and Rex Adams.

page 48:   Henri Grissino-Mayer.

page 48:   Henri Grissino-Mayer.

page 49:   John Fleck.

page 50:   Jason Hollinger.

 page 51:   Henri Grissino-Mayer.

page 52:   Lissa Heineman.

page 55:   Lissa Heineman.

page 56:   Natural Resources Conservation Service.

page 57:   Natural Resources Conservation Service.

page 57:   Natural Resources Conservation Service.

page 59:   NASA.

page 61:   NASA.

page 63:   Lissa Heineman.

page 63:   John Fleck.

page 64:   Connie Woodhouse.

page 65:   James M. Phelps.

page 66:   US Geological Survey.

page 69:   James M. Phelps, www.jmp-photography.net

page 70:   Laboratory of Tree Ring Research.

 page 71:   Connie Woodhouse.

page 72:   Connie Woodhouse.

Welcome to

Barbara Guth Worlds of Wonder

Science Series for Young Readers

Advisory Editors: David Holtby and Karen Taschek

In these engagingly written and beautifully illustrated books,
the University of New Mexico Press seeks to convey to
young readers the thrill of science as well as to inspire further
inquiry into the wonders of scientific research and discovery.

Also available in the Barbara Guth Worlds of Wonder series:

Hanging with Bats: Ecobats, Vampires, and Movie Stars
by Karen Taschek

Index